JOHN WESLEY'S SERMONS
An Introduction

JOHN WESLEY'S SERMONS
An Introduction

Albert C. Outler

Foreword by

Richard P. Heitzenrater

ABINGDON PRESS
NASHVILLE

JOHN WESLEY'S SERMONS: AN INTRODUCTION
Foreword Copyright © 1991 by Abingdon Press
Introduction reprinted from *The Works of John Wesley*, Volume 1:
Sermons I, 1–33, Copyright © 1984 by Abingdon Press

Library of Congress Cataloging-in-Publication Data

Outler, Albert Cook, 1908–1989
    John Wesley's sermons: an introduction / Albert C. Outler
        p.   cm.
    "Originally published in The works of John Wesley, volume 1: Sermons I, 1–33
(Nashville: Abingdon Press, 1984)"
    Includes bibliographical references.
    ISBN 0-687-20496-8 (alk. paper)
    1. Wesley, John, 1703–1791. 2. Preaching—History—18th century. I. Title
BX8495.W5077   1991   91-23771
251'.0092—dc20   CIP

ISBN: 0-687-20496-8

Printed in the United States of America on recycled acid-free paper

Cover illustration, from a ceramic of John Wesley by Josiah Wedgewood, reproduced
by permission of the Methodist Archives and History Committee, England

To Carla Outler

CONTENTS

FOREWORD

In the Preface to his first volume of *Sermons on Several Occasions* (1746), Wesley outlined his plan to provide the reader with 'those doctrines . . . which I embrace and teach as the essentials of true religion.' He could not have known then that his projected three volumes, completed over the following four years, would be joined by a fourth volume in 1760. Nor could he have foreseen that he would live to preach and write for thirty years beyond that and produce another seven dozen written sermons after his sixtieth birthday. Most of these sermons were collected in an eight-volume set published in his eighty-fifth year; more were collected and published posthumously.

This long and rich stream of homiletic discourse embodies more than simply the core of Wesley's doctrinal concerns. These sermons reflect Wesley's own attempts to understand and express the nature of 'the Scripture way of salvation' as experienced in his own spiritual pilgrimage that covered most of the eighteenth century. At the same time, these sermons represent a theological perspective and doctrinal position that is being hammered out and refined in the midst of a long life of continued intellectual growth and ongoing theological controversy. When Wesley's early unpublished sermons are added to the picture, the result is an outstanding record of the life and thought of an important theologian represented in his sermonic production over a period of some sixty-six years.

A full appreciation of Wesley, then, depends in part upon an adequate comprehension of this important body of material. At the same time, in order best to understand Wesley's sermons, the reader must have some comprehension of his appropriating the Christian tradition, the context of his various sermonic productions, and the relationship of the parts to the whole.

This introduction to John Wesley's sermons by Albert C. Outler is reproduced from the four-volume edition of *Sermons* in the Bicentennial Edition of *The Works of John Wesley*. That edition of the sermons is the culmination of three decades of research and reflection by Professor Outler, who through his scholarship and concern for the church became the pre-eminent interpreter of Wesley's sermons. This work is part of the larger Wesley Works Editorial Project. The Project was established in 1960 to produce a critical edition of Wesley's works that would satisfy the needs of a modern scholarship in the academy and the church. The goal of the editorial effort is not only to provide an accurate text but also to furnish extensive annotations that will illuminate the text.

This general introduction to the *Sermons* sets forth, as only Professor Outler could, the rich fabric of classical and Christian thought upon which Wesley wove his design for Christian living. It displays Wesley in the light of his sources, in the context of the preaching of his day, in the midst of controversies of his time, and in the face of continued pressures from within his own movement. Professor Outler also examines the structure and development of the sermon corpus, the relationship of the various collected editions, the role of the separately published sermons, and the place of the unpublished materials. In an important section, Outler examines Wesley's theological methodology in relation to the early, mature, and later phase of his ministry.

The text of the introduction is essentially unchanged. The frequent references to *Sermons on Several Occasions* have been shortened to *Sermons* rather than to the acronym of *SOSO* that Outler and others regretted ever having used. This separate publication has necessitated a few minor revisions in the footnotes. Cross-references within the Bicentennial Edition have been indicated by volume and page number in *Works*. The references to the forthcoming volumes have been either updated, corrected, or deleted as appropriate. Errata have been corrected when noted, both in text and footnotes. For further information about the works cited in the footnotes, see the Bibliographical Index in *Works* 4:574–650.

It is hoped that this separate edition of Professor Outler's 'Introduction' to John Wesley's sermons will enhance the appreciation for and understanding of this important body of material that is so central to the Wesleyan heritage of life and thought.

Richard P. Heitzenrater
Southern Methodist University
Dallas, Texas

1. A CAREER IN RETROSPECT

It was John Wesley's settled habit to spend his winter seasons in and around London; these seasons were interludes between his annual preaching tours throughout Great Britain during the rest of the year.[1] Sunday, December 15, 1772, found him in the Kentish village of Shoreham visiting an old, cherished friend, the Rev. Vincent Perronet, vicar of the parish church. Such a welcome respite seems to have prompted a brief moment of wistfulness. At the time, he had been leading the Methodist Revival Movement for more than a full generation; it was still flourishing despite an unending round of problems. During this peaceful day in Shoreham, he dashed off a revealing note to his brother Charles, once so active in the Revival but now happily married and comfortably ensconced in his London home on Marylebone Road. Charles was the only person in the world to whom John was prepared to open his heart freely. The letter begins with three paragraphs about current affairs and then turns, without clear connection, to a long-vanished past:

> I often cry out, *Vitae me redde priori!*[2] Let me be again an Oxford Methodist! I am often in doubt whether it would not be best for me to resume all my Oxford rules, great and small. I did then walk closely with God, and redeem the time. But what have I been doing these thirty years?

John could count on Charles to understand such a sudden uprush of nostalgia. Actually, Charles had been his brother's closest comrade during 'these thirty years'—and his most effective ally. He knew, as the others could not, how deeply John still cherished their 'former life' at Oxford, how truly a part of him still longed for a 'sweet retirement' in 'the groves of Academe'.[3] Charles had his own lively memories of the rigours and joys of

---

[1] See his letter to Mrs. Savage, Sept. 19, 1771: 'My course has been for several years as fixed as that of the sun.' See also his letter to Samuel Sparrow, July 2, 1772: '. . . In the summer months I am almost continually in motion'.

[2] 'Give me back my former life'; Horace, *Epistles*, I.vii.95. See also Wesley's *Explanatory Notes On the New Testament* (henceforth *Notes*) on Eph. 5:16 and notice the contrast here between personal self-exposure and 'business as usual'.

[3] 'Having now obtained what I had long desired, a company of friends that were as my own soul, I set up my rest, being fully determined to live and die in this sweet retirement.' ('A Short History of the People Called Methodists', §4; see *Works* 9:425–503. See also the reference to *inter sylvas academicas* in Wesley's letter to 'John Smith', June 25, 1746, and in

life in the Holy Club from 1729 to 1735; he could recall how popular a university preacher his brother had been from 1730 to 1735, despite much snide merriment about the enthusiasm of the 'Methodists', 'Bible Moths', 'Supererogation men', etc.[4] But he also remembered, more realistically than John, how barren of happiness and holiness those years had been, how ill-fated their Georgia mission, how unpromising their prospects in England after their return. He could have reminded John of how exciting it had been, after 1738, when their new-found experience of faith and their latent talents for communicating saving faith to 'plain people' had added a new impetus to the revival movements already stirring in many parts of Britain. Thus, he would have understood how to interpret John's passing spasm of nostalgia; he knew that only a part of John could have ever been content again with that *vita priori* in Oxford.

Moreover, despite a deepening dismay about his brother's irregular 'churchmanship', Charles had a clearer view than anyone else of the positive achievements of the three decades since 1738.[5] He had himself become the poet laureate of the Methodist people and a rousing preacher in his own right.[6] His main ecclesial concern had been to keep the Methodists safely within the Church of England as a 'religious society'. As the threat of 'separation' had loomed larger, however, he had fled the Conference of 1755, protesting what he foresaw in an anguished poetical *Epistle* to his brother.[7] In 1756 he had settled in London and, thereafter, had loos-

---

'Some Remarks on Article X of Mr. Maty's New Review for December, 1784', §6, in the *Arminian Magazine* 8 (1785):152 (*Works* 9:522–26). See also a similar quotation from Horace in *A Farther Appeal*, Part III, §III.18 (*Works* 11:303). For a reference to 'beloved obscurity', see Sermon 112, *On Laying the Foundation of the New Chapel*, §I.5 and n.)

[4] At the invitation of Bishop Potter, Wesley had preached an ordination sermon in Christ Church Cathedral, Sept. 19, 1730, just two years after his own ordination as priest. Thereafter, until he left for Georgia, his invitations to preach before the university far exceeded the normal rotation.

[5] None of Charles's diaries, journal, or letters was published in his lifetime. A biography based on his surviving papers, preserved by his daughter, Sarah, was written by Thomas Jackson in 1841. Jackson then edited and published *The Journal of the Rev. Charles Wesley, M. A. . . . with Selections from his Correspondence and Poetry*, 2 vols., (London, 1849); henceforth CWJ. A collection of *Sermons by the Late Rev. Charles Wesley, A. M.* was published in 1816.

[6] See John Wesley's letter to Charles, June 27, 1766: 'In connexion I beat you; but in strong, pointed sentences you beat me.' John Whitehead said Charles's sermons were more 'awakening and useful' than John's; see his *Life of the Rev. John Wesley*, 2 vols. (London, 1793–1796), 1:292. Henry Moore's assessment was that 'John's preaching was all principles; Charles's was all aphorisms'; see E. H. Sugden, ed., *Wesley's Standard Sermons*, 2 vols. (London, 1921), 1:69; henceforth 'Sugden'.

[7] *An Epistle to the Reverend Mr. John Wesley. By Charles Wesley, Presbyter of the Church of*

ened his connection with the Conference. His own retrospective would, therefore, have been different from John's, and yet he would have realized his brother's unstated appeal that his unique ministry, 'these thirty years', had not been in vain.

There was, of course, a voluminous public record of that ministry (1738-72). Wesley's own version of those years had appeared in the successive *Extracts from the Journal of the Rev. John Wesley*,[8] in *A Short History of Methodism* (1765), and in a series of *Appeals to Men of Reason and Religion* (1743-45).[9] Besides, there had been a steady stream of critics of Methodism, from Josiah Tucker's 'Three Queries' in the *Weekly Miscellany* (1739), and *A Brief History of the Principles of Methodism* (1742), down to the furious controversy with the Calvinists that was still roiling.[10] No other religious leader in his century had provoked so varied an array of opponents, from clerics (and a few laymen), to the Bishops of Exeter and Gloucester.[11] On that Sunday at Shoreham, Perronet was entertaining the most widely exposed private person in England.[12]

His career as a truly effective evangelist ran back to 1739 when, with grave misgivings, he had joined George Whitefield (former colleague in the Holy Club and fellow missionary to America) in a preaching mission to the poor on the outskirts of Bristol.[13] This reluctant venture had followed a

---

England (London, 1755).

[8] Extracts 1-14 had been published by 1772; seven were to follow.

[9] *Works* 9:367-72 and 11:45-325.

[10] See the Calvinist onslaught in *The Gospel Magazine* and the polemical attacks of Augustus Toplady (*A Caveat against Unsound Doctrines*, 1770; *A Letter to the Rev. Mr. John Wesley relative to his pretended Abridgment of Zanchius on Predestination*, 1770; *More Work for Mr. John Wesley*, 1772) and Richard Hill (*Pietas Oxoniensis*, 1768; *A Conversation between Richard Hill, Esq., The Rev. Mr. Madan, and Father Walsh, the Superior of a Convent of English Benedictine Monks at Paris . . . Relative to Some Doctrinal Minutes advanced by the Rev. Mr. John Wesley and Others at a Conference held in London, Aug. 7, 1770, 1772; A Review of all the Doctrines Taught by the Rev. Mr. John Wesley*, 1772). The controversy continued fiercely, as in *Logica Wesleiensis: Or the Farrago Double-Distilled* (1773).

[11] See George Lavington, *The Enthusiasm of Methodists and Papists Compared. . .* , Parts I and II (1749); Part III (1751). See also the spirited replies of Whitefield, Vincent Perronet, and John Wesley. See also William Warburton, *The Doctrine of Grace: Or, the Office and Operations of the Holy Spirit Vindicated from the Insults of Infidelity and the Abuses of Fanaticism* [i.e., Methodism]. . . , 2 vols. (1763). For the whole panoply of anti-Methodist polemic, see Richard Green, *Anti-Methodist Publications Issued During the Eighteenth Century* (London, 1902).

[12] See Joseph G. Wright, 'Notes on Some Portraits of John Wesley', in *The Proceedings of the Wesley Historical Society* (1898-), 3 (1902):185-92; henceforth *WHS*.

[13] John Wesley, *Journal*, in preparation by W. Reginald Ward and Richard P. Heitzenrater as vols. 18-24 of *Works*, Mar. 10-Apr. 8, 1739; henceforth *JWJ*, with citations by date. For volumes of *JWJ* not yet available in *Works*, see Nehemiah Curnock, ed., *The*

succession of climactic experiences strung out over the entire year of 1738. Even before that, Wesley had pressed his quest for a personal assurance of God's pardoning grace in reaction to challenges from the Moravians and Salzburgers in Georgia. Following his return to England there had been an intense two-month span of soul searching that had reached a climax in the famous experience in 'a society in Aldersgate Street' on the evening of May 24th.[14] This, in turn, had prompted a pilgrimage to the Moravian heartland (Marienborn and Herrnhut) that had enabled him to make a probing study of Moravian life and doctrine—and of the personality cult that had grown up around their leader, Count Ludwig von Zinzendorf.[15] Then, in the following October, he had been shaken, yet again, by his discovery of Jonathan Edwards's *Faithful Narrative of a Surprising Work of God in New England* (1736).[16] The cumulative effect of this series of experiences was to drive him back to his own Anglican heritage, specifically to the Edwardian *Homilies* of 1547. There he had found a resolution to his doctrinal perplexities to match his new-found sense of assurance. This had prompted him to extract from Homilies 1–4 an abridgement, which he then published and used as a theological charter throughout his whole career.[17] The end product of this series of conversions was a radical shift in his self-understanding of 'the order of salvation'—away from holy living as a precondition to saving faith, to faith itself as the threshold of any valid experience of true holiness.

When he began his field preaching in 1739, Wesley had known next to nothing of the scattered revival movements elsewhere in England.[18] He

---

Journal of the Rev. John Wesley, 8 vols. (London, 1909–16); henceforth 'Curnock.'

[14] See the carefully composed account of this in the *Journal* entry for that date; note the review of his spiritual pilgrimage from childhood to the very moment ('about a quarter before nine') when, as he says, 'I felt my heart strangely warmed. . . ; and an assurance was given me that [Christ] had taken away my sins, even mine, and saved me from the law of sin and death.' The parallel here with St. Augustine's famous account of his conversion in the Milanese garden is clearly not unconscious; see *Confessions*, VIII. vii–xii (§§16–30).

[15] See Edward Langton, *History of the Moravian Church* (New York, 1956); J. E. Hutton, *A History of the Moravian Church*, 2nd edition (London, 1909); W. G. Addison, *The Renewed Church of the United Brethren, 1722–1930* (London, 1932); Daniel Benham, *Memoirs of James Hutton* (London, 1856). See also, Wesley's letter of Aug. 8, 1740, 'To the Church of God at Herrnhut in Upper Lusatia', *Works* 26:24–30.

[16] See below, p. 48.

[17] See JWJ, Nov. 12, 1738: 'In the following week, I began more narrowly to inquire what the doctrine of the Church of England is concerning the much-controverted point of justification by faith; and the sum of what I found in the Homilies I extracted and printed for the use of others'—*The Doctrine of Salvation, Faith, and Good Works* (1738); it went through thirteen editions in Wesley's lifetime.

[18] See J. D. Walsh, 'Origins of the Evangelical Revival', in G. V. Bennet and J. D. Walsh, eds., *Essays in Modern English Church History* (London, 1966), 132–62.

was, however, aware of Whitefield's exciting work in and around Bristol, and he must have known of the tradition of the Quaker and Baptist field preachers who had ministered in these outlying districts during the turmoils of the Restoration.[19] What no one had counted on was that the upshot of his field preaching would be the discovery of his true vocation as an evangelist and the launching of a revival movement destined to eclipse the others both in its scope and staying power. Wesley's 'Methodism' quickly took on a character of its own—a 'connexion' of religious societies within the Church of England, with 'class-meetings' for prayer, study, and mutual help, together with active philanthropic programmes for the needy.[20] For 'these thirty years', then, Wesley had directed and governed this movement, and would continue to do so till his death in 1791. And yet, despite his gifts as leader and organizer, it was his impression that he had never *planned* the Methodist Revival. He had instead been gathered up into it and swept along by what seemed to him the clear leadings of divine providence.[21] It was Wesley's way to *re*-act to opportunities and openings as they came along rather than to preform the future by his own design. From childhood, he had had a sense of being set apart for a special destiny, 'a brand plucked out of the burning';[22] he had also come to lend special meanings to the metaphors of 'fire', 'flame', and 'light'.[23]

Any proper answer, then, to his rhetorical question about 'these thirty years' would have amounted to a survey of the middle third of his career. Among many other things, it would have included the story of his organiza-

---

[19] See the commemorative plaques on Hanham Mount near Bristol: 'Dedicated to the Field Preachers, 1658-1739'; [they] 'often forded the flooded Avon and risked imprisonment and death for their faith'; 'Out of the Wood came Light.' What is not so easy to explain is the absence of any reference to Whitefield, Wesley, or their ministries, on any of the plaques.

[20] Note the similarities and differences between this new United Society and the older ones described by Josiah Woodward in *An Account of the Rise and Progress of the Religious Societies in the City of London* (1698). See also John S. Simon, *John Wesley and the Religious Societies* (London, 1923).

[21] See his letter to James Hutton, June 7, 1739: 'I enforced (as not my choice, but the providence of God, directed me) those words of Isaiah. . . .'; a letter to Charles, Sept. 28, 1769: 'All our lives and all God's dealings with us have been extraordinary from the beginning. . . .'; his annual *Minutes* for 1765 (Q. [26]): 'God . . . thrust us out, utterly against our will, to raise an holy people'; see also Sermon 107, 'On God's Vineyard', §II.3.

[22] This was associated with his experience of a dramatic rescue from a fire that destroyed the Epworth Rectory in 1709. For the story of that rescue in Susanna Wesley's words, see her letter of Aug. 24, 1709, to the Rev. Mr. Hoole, in Henry Moore, *The Life of the Rev. John Wesley* (London, 1824, 1825), 1:112-14; for Wesley's remembrance of it as told to Moore, see 1:114-15; see also his MS Journal for Mar. 7, 1737, and JWJ, Feb. 7, 1750.

[23] See James Downey, *Eighteenth Century Pulpit* (Oxford, 1969), 221.

tion of the United Methodist Societies and his employment of laymen as 'Assistants'; this would have explained the origins and unique functions of the 'Annual Conference' of his clerical and lay brethren (with himself as host and president). It had also included an extensive programme of editing and publishing that was still going forward.[24] In 1772 he was deeply engaged with the only edition of his *Works* that he himself would collect and order: thirty-two volumes headed by fifty-three sermons in Volumes 1–4.[25] Throughout, he had been engaged in a relentless succession of controversies in which he had undertaken to clarify, develop, and defend his theological ideas. It was, therefore, natural enough that, with all these cumulative pressures, he would have been prompted wistfully to recall that quieter, more ordered 'former life' at Oxford.

We know less about John Wesley, as person and preacher, from those earlier days than from his later years of fame and notoriety. There are remembrances of him from his Oxford days: of his charming manners and sprightly conversation.[26] But a rather different impression comes from the reports of William Stephens, secretary to the Trustees for the Georgia Colony, who visited him in Savannah just as his troubled ministry there was nearing its inglorious end.[27] The Earl of Egmont, a Trustee for the Georgia Colony, remembered Wesley as 'an odd mixture of a man'; he and many of the other trustees were clearly dissatisfied with his work as chaplain.[28]

With increasing fame, however, there had come more notice from competent observers, but notoriety, too, not to mention the swelling flood of portraits, busts, medallions, and relics (in a burgeoning hero-cult).[29]

---

[24] See T. W. Herbert, *John Wesley as Editor and Author* (Princeton, 1940). Wesley's theological biases and editorial methods may be studied at firsthand in his *Christian Library* and the *Arminian Magazine*.

[25] By 1772 sixteen vols. had been published; vols. 17–25 appeared in 1773, 26–32 in 1774.

[26] See Samuel Badcock's description of Wesley as a 'very sensible and acute collegian, baffling every man by the subtleties of logic, and laughing at them for being so easily routed; a young fellow of the finest classical taste, of the most liberal and manly sentiments', whose pen could produce surprisingly 'gay and sprightly' verse (*Westminster Magazine*, Apr. 1774, p. 180). See also V. H. H. Green, *The Young Mr. Wesley: A Study of John Wesley at Oxford* (London, 1961), chs. 4, 6, 10–11.

[27] See William Stephens, *Journal of the Proceedings in Georgia* (London, 1742), 1:10, 11–12, 14–15, 19–20, 30–31, 36–37, 40–41, 45–46, 53, 65, 234–35; this last entry notes Stephen's dismay at discovering the parish register 'filled with the names of communicants at the Sacraments . . . instead of an account of births and burials'.

[28] *Diary of Viscount Percival, Afterwards First Earl of Egmont*, R. A. Roberts, ed., 3 vols. (London, 1920–23), 2:481 (Apr. 26, 1738).

[29] E.g., his silver buckles were passed on from family to family till finally they were

Howel Harris wrote approvingly of a sermon of Wesley's that he had heard in May, 1743.[30] From many sources there are two of uncommon interest and trustworthiness. Just three years before John's letter to Charles, a visiting Swedish professor, Johan Henrik Liden, of Uppsala, had met the elder Wesley in London (on Sunday, Oct. 15, 1769). His report to his friends back home is revealing:

> Today I learned for the first time to know Mr. John Wesley, so well known here in England, and called the spiritual father of the so-called 'Methodists'. He arrived home yesterday from his summer journey to Ireland, where he has visited his people. He preached today at the forenoon service in the Methodist Chapel in Spitalfields for an audience of more than 4,000 people. His text was Luke 1:68. The sermon was short but eminently evangelical. He has no great oratorical gifts, no outward appearance, but he speaks clear and pleasant. After the Holy Communion (which in all English churches is held with closed doors at the end of the preaching service, when none but the communicants usually are present, and which here was celebrated very orderly and pathetic), I went forward to shake hands with Mr. Wesley . . . and was received by him in his usual amiable and friendly way. He is a small, thin old man, with his own long and straight hair, and looks as the worst country curate in Sweden, but has learning as a bishop and a zeal for the glory of God which is quite extraordinary. His talk is very agreeable. . . . He is the personification of piety, and he seems to me as a living representation of the loving Apostle John. The old man Wesley is already 66 years, but very lively and exceedingly industrious. I also spoke with his younger brother, Mr. Charles Wesley, also a Methodist minister and a pious man, but neither in learning or activity can he be compared with the older brother.[31]

A later account comes from the well-known evangelical historian, Thomas Haweis, who had collected all eyewitness evidence available to him:

> John Wesley was of the inferior size [five feet, three inches], his visage marked with intelligence, singularly neat and plain in his dress, a little cast in his eye observable upon particular occasions, upright, graceful, and remarkably active. His understanding, naturally excellent and acute, was highly stored with the attainments of literature, and he possessed a fund of anec-

---

bequeathed to the museum in Wesley's House on City Road, London; see T. Francis Glasson in *WHS* 33 (1962):177–78. There was even a vogue for 'Wesley tablecloths', etc.; see *WHS* 37 (1969):31–33. No other Englishman of his time had had as many likenesses struck off—but with such wide differences between them that it is impossible to decide on one above the others as the most accurate.

[30] See his letter of May 12th to George Whitefield: 'Last Sunday I heard Bro. John Wesley preach upon the seventh of the Romans. He was very sweet and loving, and seemed to have his heart honestly bent on drawing the poor souls to Christ' (Curnock 3:77n).

[31] *WHS* 17 (1929):2.

dote and history that rendered his company as entertaining as instructive. His mode of address in public was chaste and solemn, though not illumined with those coruscations of eloquence which marked, if I may use that expression, the discourses of his rival, George Whitefield. But there was a divine simplicity, a zeal, a venerableness in his manner which commanded attention and never forsook him in his latest years. When at fourscore he retained all the freshness of vigorous old age, his health was remarkably preserved amidst a scene of labour and perpetual exertions of mind and body to which few would have been equal. Never man possessed greater personal influence over the people connected with him, nor was it an easy task to direct so vast a machine [the Methodist Societies] when amidst so many hundred wheels in motion some moved eccentrically and hardly yielded to the impulse of the mainspring. I need not speak of the exemplariness of his life. Too many eyes were upon him to admit of his halting, nor could his weight have been maintained a moment longer than the fullest conviction impressed his people that he was eminently favoured as a saint of God and as distinguished for his holy walk as for his vast abilities, indefatigible and singular usefulness.[32]

Thus, at the time he was giving voice to his passing nostalgia, John Wesley had already set a notable mark on English Christianity, had brought new form and power to popular religion, had altered and enriched the theological climate of his time. This harvest of a unique career had come, more than he or the others realized, from a radical role-reversal from his original identity as academic don and regular cleric to a virtual identification with the English underclass. They, in turn, had accepted him as one of their own and yet also as their spiritual director, theological mentor, and pastoral counselor. His unconventional ministry had given them not only a new hope of grace and salvation *in this life* but also a new sense of human dignity, also *in this life*. Judged by almost any norm, it had been a unique career, and in 1772 it still had two remarkable decades left.[33]

He had been born in an out-of-the-way Lincolnshire village in an England still shaken by the shocks of civil war and dynastic violence. He had grown up amidst the dying throes of the feudal system in the English

---

[32] Thomas Haweis, *An Impartial and Succinct History of the Rise and Declension and Revival of the Church of Christ* (London, 1807), 2:435–36. For a thoughtful disciple's considered (and generally reliable) retrospect on Wesley as person and preacher, see Whitehead, *John Wesley* 2:466–68. There is a useful collection of other eyewitness accounts in R. Denny Urlin, *A Churchman's Life of Wesley* (London, 1880), Appendix XIII, 'Portraiture and Character', 334–46.

[33] See W. E. H. Lecky's fulsome account of Wesley and Methodism in *A History of England in the Eighteenth Century* (New York, 1892), 3:37–153. See also Charles Grant Robertson, *England Under the Hanoverians* (London, 1911); and Basil Williams, *The Whig Supremacy, 1714–1760* (Oxford, 1939).

Church and civil state, nowhere more vividly described than in Gilbert Burnet's classic autobiography, which Wesley had read in Oxford.[34] His career had been cast in a century of bewildering transitions in English society: political and cultural changes that gave the label 'Georgian' to an epoch, social and economic changes that prepared the way for the cruelly unequal prosperity of the late eighteenth century. He had done more than survive these transitions passively; he had himself been one of the forces of significant change. His firsthand acquaintance with the English masses, and with Britain generally, was unmatched—certainly by any churchman.

Wesley's backward glance, then, was obviously less concerned with onward events of his career than with their meaning and lasting value. It was a rare lapse of self-confidence in the midst of conflict in which he usually moved serenely. He realized that many of his Anglican critics saw nothing but confusion in his theological endeavours to synthesize the two rival traditions of evangelical faith and 'holy living'. The Calvinists had denounced him, not only as 'Arminian', but also as a 'Papist', a 'Presbyterian Papist', 'a puny tadpole in divinity'.[35] His steadfast reply to all this was an unwavering profession of loyalty to the Church of England as defined by her Homilies, the Articles of Religion, and the Book of Common Prayer. Very late in life, with his movement headed toward eventual separation, he would go on repeating his old profession: 'I declare once more that I live and die a member of the Church of England, and that none who regard my judgment or advice will ever separate from it.'[36] He never saw himself as a

---

[34] *History of His Own Time, 1643–1715*, 2 vols. (1724, 1734); Wesley had read the first volume in 1725.

[35] His ablest Anglican critics were Josiah Tucker and 'John Smith', for whose correspondence with Wesley see *Works* 26:153–294, *passim*. See also Thomas Church, *Remarks on the Rev. Mr. John Wesley's Last Journal* (1745).

For the charges of 'papism', see *JWJ*, Oct. 30, 1743; Aug. 27, 1739; Apr. 11, 1740; and Sept. 24, 1742. Some of his opponents were even more colourful in their epithets; see 'An Old Fox Tarr'd and Feather'd', Augustus Toplady, *Works* (1837), 762. In a pamphlet of no more than forty pages, Rowland Hill calls Wesley 'a designing wolf', 'a dealer in stolen words', 'as unprincipled as a rook and as silly as a jackdaw', 'a grey-headed enemy of all righteousness', 'a wretch' guilty of 'wilful, gross and abominable untruth', 'a venal profligate', 'a wicked slanderer', 'an apostate miscreant', 'libeller', 'crafty slanderer', 'an unfeeling reviler', 'a liar of the most gigantic magnitude', 'a Solomon in a cassock', 'a disappointed *Orlando Furioso*', 'Pope John', 'this living lump of inconsistencies', etc.; see *Imposture Detected and the Dead Vindicated: in a Letter to a Friend* (1777).

[36] See 'Farther Thoughts on Separation from the Church', §7, in *Arminian Magazine* 13 (1790):216 (*Works* 9:538–40); see his letter to *The Dublin Chronicle*, June 2, 1789 ('In my youth I was not only a member of the Church of England but a bigot to it.'); his letter to Henry Moore, May 6, 1788 ('I am a Church of England man; . . . in the Church I will live and die, unless I am thrust out.'); to Joseph Taylor, Jan. 16, 1783, and to John Mason,

rebel, even though the blithe irregularities in his churchmanship left the impression that, although he was certainly *in* the Church of England as defined by her tradition, he was never altogether *of* it, as defined by her eighteenth century self-understanding.[37]

The evidence about his personal disposition and temperament is curiously inconsistent. Aaron Seymour speaks of him as 'cheerful'; Richard Viney, who knew him better, commented on his 'choleric complexion'. His sister Emily complained that he had reined his feelings so tightly that he regarded 'natural affections as a great weakness if not a sin'.[38] Even so, he shed resentments easily and was honestly averse to controversy unless sorely provoked. By the same token, though, he reacted to criticism with the instincts of a born debater, with a habit of logic-chopping and a notable gift for sarcasm.[39] And yet, one of his wisest and most discerning friends, Alexander Knox (himself a mentor to Pusey, Keble, and Newman), said of him: 'He was, in truth, the most perfect specimen of *moral happiness* which I ever saw.' Yet Knox spoke also of the 'sudden revolutions of [Wesley's] mind', 'his proneness to attribute to the Spirit of God what might more reasonably be resolved into natural emotions.'[40] This throws a flood of

---

Mar. 22, 1772. See also Sermon 121, 'Prophets and Priests', §18.

The term 'Anglican' was not in common use in Wesley's time, but the basic equation of the terms 'national', 'establishment', 'Church of England men', and 'Anglican' had already been made by Joseph Glanvill, *A Seasonable Defence of Preaching* (1678), 74–75. Later, the Tractarians would co-opt the phrase and associate it with the medieval notions of an *ecclesia anglicana* as a regional catholic church. For the propriety of the label 'Anglican' in Wesley's case, see Frank Baker, *John Wesley and the Church of England* (Nashville and New York, 1970), 6.

[37] For a comprehensive analysis of this complex relationship, see Baker, chs. 14–17, 'Epilogue', and Appendix (326–40).

[38] See his letter to 'Mrs. Harper', June 30, 1743, and note Wesley's surprised denial of such a charge. See also A. C. H. Seymour, *Life and Times of Selina, Countess of Huntingdon*, 2 vols. (London, 1840), 1:58, and 'Richard Viney's Diary', May 29, 1744, in *WHS* 14 (1924):198. For other comments on the question of 'inordinate affection', see Sermons 14, *The Repentance of Believers*, §I.5; and 84, *The Important Question*, §III.10; and his letters to Ann Bolton, Nov. 28, 1772, to Sarah Mallet, Oct. 6, 1787 and Mar. 11, 1788, and to Adam Clarke, Jan. 3, 1791.

[39] For his unprovoked attack on his former mentor, William Law, see A. Keith Walker, *William Law: His Life and Thought* (London, 1973), especially 127–39; for his anti-Calvinist polemic in *Predestination Calmly Considered* (1752), *passim*, and his debate with John Taylor of Norwich in *The Doctrine of Original Sin: According to Scripture, Reason, and Experience* (1757).

[40] See Knox's 'Remarks on the Life and Character of John Wesley', in Robert Southey, *The Life of Wesley*, new edition, ed. C. C. Southey, with Knox's 'Remarks' (London, 1864), 2:344, 339. In defending Wesley from the charge of vanity, however, Knox wrote: 'Great minds are not vain: and [Wesley's] was a great mind, if any mind can be made great by

light on the twists and turns of his personal life: e.g., the Sophy Hopkey affair in Georgia, the tragic breach with George Whitefield, his resort to pious sortilege in making important decisions, his aborted courtship of Grace Murray, his unhappy marriage—and so on and on.[41]

He was a truly humble man, at home with great and small; he loved and was loved by little children everywhere.[42] But he also commanded respect, even from the mobs, and was immensely popular with many of Britain's 'plain people'. He was a High Church Tory who made it a point to wear his clerical vestments whenever he preached, even in the fields.[43] He also understood himself as an Anglican theologian with a special mission to teach the masses, well content for his teachings to be judged by the immemorial Anglican canons of 'Scripture, reason, and Christian antiquity'.[44] Into the bargain, however, he was also a decisive influence in the reformation of manners that had already been noticed before the century was out.[45]

---

distinterested benevolence, spotless purity, and simple devotedness.' *Thirty Years' Correspondence between John Jebb and Alexander Knox*, 2nd edition (London, 1836), 2:460.

[41] See Wesley's MS account of his relations with Sophy Hopkey, Mar. 1736 to Mar. 12, 1737, in the Methodist Archives, John Rylands University Library of Manchester. For the breach with Whitefield, see Southey, ch. 11, Luke Tyerman, *Life and Times of John Wesley*, 3 vols. (New York, 1872), 1:311-25, and for Whitefield's side *George Whitefield's Journals*, Iain Murray, ed. (London, 1960), Appendix III, 563-88. For a MS account of the Grace Murray affair, see British Library, Add. MS Sermon 7119; see J. A. Leger, *John Wesley's Last Love* (London, 1910). For samplings of his use of lots, see JWJ, Mar. 4, 1737 (see diary), Mar. 28, 1739, and also his open letter to Thomas Church, June 17, 1746 (§IV.3-4), *Works* 9:80-122.

[42] Charles Atmore recalls a sermon to children at Bolton, 'literally composed and delivered in words of not more than two syllables' (Curnock, 8:63n.); see also Tyerman, *John Wesley*, 3:472; and Banning's account in his *Memoir*, (*see WHS* 4 (1904):119-20). Matthias Joyce, one of Wesley's preachers, recalled the first time he heard Wesley preach (in 1773) and added: 'What endeared him still more to me was seeing him stoop to kiss a little child that stood on the stairs.' *Wesley's Veterans*, 7 vols. (London, 1912-1914), 7:191.

[43] See JWJ, Sept. 9, 1743 (during a visit to the wild country of St. Hilary Downs in Cornwall): 'The Downs I found, but no congregation, neither man, woman, nor child. But by that [time] I had put on my gown and cassock about an hundred gathered themselves together.' Frederick Gill, *In the Steps of John Wesley*, (New York, 1963), 149-50, gives an account of an old man at Hull who remembered Wesley as 'a bonny little man, with such a canny nice face', wearing 'knee breeches, black stockings, and buckles on his shoes, with his bonny white hair hanging on his black gown, and a clean white thing like two sark necks, hanging down on his breast'.

[44] See 'To the Reader', §4, in *Works* (1771), vol. 1.

[45] See Bernard Semmel, *The Methodist Revolution* (New York, 1973), chs. 1-4; see also Dorothy George, *London Life in the Eighteenth Century* (London, 1930), 16-17: 'By the end of the [eighteenth] century we are in a different world. . . . We see a revolution comparable with conversion.' See Christopher Hill, *Reformation to Industrial Revolution*, vol. 2 in *The*

Wesley's character, then, was complex and paradoxical in many ways. And yet there were two wholly consistent concerns running throughout his ministry after 1739 and clearly mirrored in his sermons. One of these was his special sense of calling to an 'extraordinary ministry' to the masses beyond the reach of the 'ordinary ministries' of a state church so hobbled by the suspensions of her Convocation that she could not respond to new needs created by out-dated parish boundaries, conflicting jurisdictions, and tragic human dislocations.[46] Even before his own Revival had been launched, Wesley had claimed, 'I look upon *all the world* as *my parish*; thus far I mean, that in whatever part of it I am I judge it meet, right, and my bounden duty, to declare unto all that are willing to hear the glad tidings of salvation. This is the work which I know God has called me to. And sure I am that his blessing attends it.'[47] Thus, he felt free not only to preach wherever he found an auditory, but he was equally concerned to organize his converts into religious societies and to enlist them in the ongoing tasks of Christian nurture in mutually sustaining small groups.[48]

The other clue to Wesley's inner consistency, despite all his 'sudden revolutions', may be seen in his intensely practical concern with the order of salvation in the Christian life. The controlling theological inquiry throughout his life was into the meaning of becoming and being a Christian in all the aspects of Christian existence. Here one may find the genuine integration of what seemed to some of his critics as nothing better than 'a medley of . . . Calvinism, Arminianism, Montanism, Quakerism, Quietism, all thrown together'.[49] This preoccupation with the *ordo salutis* and his cumulative insights into its wholeness may be recognized in all the developments in his preaching and in his personal pilgrimage as well.[50]

Pelican Economic History of Britain (Harmondsworth, England, 1971), 276; note Hill's complaint that the Methodists 'liberated people without democratizing society'; see also John D. Gay, *The Geography of Religion in England* (London, 1971), 146.

[46] The Whigs had prorogued both Convocations of Canterbury and York in 1717; they were reconvened briefly in 1741, and then silenced until 1852 (for Canterbury; 1861 for York). This had the effect of freezing the church's administration in its *status quo* during a crucial period of rapid social change.

[47] See letter of Mar. 28 (?), 1739; long tradition has this letter dated as Mar. 20 and as written to James Hervey, but incorrectly. It was addressed to some clergyman (possibly John Clayton) who had already raised the issue of Wesley's right to invade other men's parishes without invitation (see *Works* 25:614, 616). See also the carefully edited account of Wesley's conversation with Bishop Butler of Bristol, Aug. 16, 1739, in *WHS* 42 (1979):93-100.

[48] See Thomas Oden, *The Intensive Group Experience: The New Pietism* (Philadelphia, 1972), 56-88.

[49] *The Principles of a Methodist*, §30 (*Works* 9:47-66), in response to Josiah Tucker's *Brief History*, 39.

[50] On this point, a careful comparison and contrast between Wesley and Søren Kierke-

By 1772, therefore, there was no way back to that 'former life' of Wesley; there never had been, really. He had had a slow start, and one or two false starts. But, finally, he had found his unique calling, and his sermons (early, middle, and late) are mirrors to that.

gaard might be very fruitful; see Kierkegaard's stress on 'becoming a Christian', generally, and especially in *Training in Christianity*, Walter Lowrie, tr. (London, 1941).

2. THE PREACHER AND HIS PREACHING

For Wesley it was preaching that defined his vocation preeminently.[1] This was the principal means of gathering converts into Christian fellowship and of nurturing them in it. 'In the first church', as he believed, 'the primary business of apostles, evangelists, and bishops was to preach the Word of God';[2] he had taken this as his own chief business. Even before he left England for Georgia, he could say, unpompously, to John Burton, 'My tongue is a devoted thing.'[3] His first venture into field preaching had wrenched all his habits and preferences out of shape,[4] but the startling response had overcome his reluctance. His experiences in Kingswood and Moorfields had convinced him that this 'extraordinary' ministry, beyond the confines of parish and campus, had become his special ministry.

He had already learned to preach extempore in Oxford.[5] After 1739 he was even more earnestly convinced that preaching, to be effective, must be an interpersonal encounter between the preacher and his hearers. Hence, he believed that oral preaching was the norm. Written sermons could only be regarded as either preparatory for more effective oral utterance or else distillates of it: the written word as substitute for personal presence. However, he saw an important difference between the principal aims of an oral and a written sermon: the former is chiefly for *proclamation* and invitation; the latter is chiefly for *nurture* and reflection. Many of Wesley's favourite

---

[1] See JWJ, July 28, 1757: 'About noon I preached at Woodseats, in the evening at Sheffield. I do indeed *live* by preaching!'

[2] *Notes*, Acts 6:2.

[3] Letter, Oct. 10, 1735.

[4] JWJ, Apr. 2, 1739; his first experiment of preaching in the open air had been on the deck of the ship *Simmonds*, Oct. 19, 1735, but that had clearly been exceptional.

[5] The Puritan traditions of extempore prayer and preaching go back at least to their early leaders like William Fulke (1538–89); see his *Brief and Plain Declaration Concerning the Desires of all Those Faithful Ministers that Have and Do Seek for the Discipline and Reformation of the Church of England* (1584), in Leonard J. Trinterud, ed., *Elizabethan Puritanism*, A Library of Protestant Thought (New York, 1971), 267-69. The first record of Wesley's extempore preaching is in his diary, Nov. 10, 1734: 'Began preaching extempore on the Beatitudes'—in the Castle at Oxford. Much later (JWJ, Jan. 28, 1776), he would (incorrectly) remember that his first such experiment was in the year 1735, in All Hallows Church, Lombard Street, London: 'This was the first time that, having no notes about me, I preached extempore.'

texts for oral preaching do not appear at all in the corpus of his written sermons and vice versa. This fact, plus the enormous range of his oral sermon texts, disposes of the suggestion that Wesley had a limited repertory of memorized discourses which he merely repeated to different auditories. As far as we can tell, the doctrinal substance of the two genres was identical; and when Wesley finally resorted to a *written* corpus as an extension of his wider ministry, it was designated for his own people as well as for any others who also might be interested.

His compulsion to preach wherever opportunity offered had driven him into the fields.[6] His self-justification here was twofold. The first was his 'right to preach anywhere' (*ius predicandi ubique*) that he understood as having been implied in his Oxford ordination.[7] 'Being ordained as Fellow of a College [he had claimed in 1739], I was not limited to any particular cure, but have an indeterminate commission, to preach the Word of God in any part of the Church of England.'[8] Later, he would be even more specific: 'I . . . was ordained as a member of that "College of Divines" [i.e., Lincoln] (so our statutes express it) "founded to overturn all heresies, and defend the Catholic faith".'[9] Wesley's second justification rested on the distinction, already mentioned, between the settled parish ministry (*ministerium ordinarium*) and the validity, *in exceptional circumstances*, of an irregular and informal ministry (*ministerium extraordinarium*). This, as we shall see,

---

[6] Beginning in 1738, Wesley began to be barred from many regular pulpits (e.g., St. Lawrence Jewry; St. Katherine Cree; St. John's, Wapping; St. Benet, Paul's Wharf; St. Antholin), as he explained to Samuel Walker (Sept. 19, 1757), for preaching 'repentance and remission of sins and [for] insist[ing] that we are justified by faith. . . . (I say for *this*: as yet there was no field preaching). And this exclusion occasioned our preaching elsewhere, with the other irregularities that followed.' Later, he would become 'an honourable man', welcomed into many pulpits, so that he would write, 'I have more invitations to preach in churches than I can accept of' (JWJ, Jan. 19, 1783). In a single four-year span (1780-84) he was invited into more than fifty regular pulpits and barred from only one thereafter. For a list of churches where Wesley preached again after having been shut out of these pulpits in 1738-39, see A. Skevington Wood, *The Burning Heart: John Wesley, Evangelist* (Grand Rapids, 1967), 201.

[7] Hastings Rashdall, *The Universities of Europe in the Middle Ages*, Frederick Maurice Powicke and Alfred Brotherston Emden, eds. (Oxford, 1936), 3:136, notes that the Chancellor of Oxford had by tradition the right to 'license preachers to preach in every diocese in England'.

[8] See p. 22, n. 47 above, Wesley's interview with Bishop Butler.

[9] *Farther Appeal*, Part I, §VI.9 (*Works* 11:183). The heresies first here in view were those of Wycliffe and the Lollards. See Wesley's *Principles of a Methodist Farther Explain'd* (1746), §III.5, *Works* 9:160-237. See also Felix Makower, *The Constitutional History and Constitution of the Church of England* (London, 1895), 491, on Canon 33 of 'The Canons of 1604'. Wesley also seems to have believed that he had the personal support of King George himself in his irregularities; see JWJ, Sept. 3, 1750.

was a tradition that ran back into the Middle Ages and still seemed warranted in the special circumstances of the eighteenth century. These two different types of ministry, in Wesley's view, need not be rivals; they ought to be partners. As an itinerant, he rarely preached during 'church hours'; there were other times when people might conveniently be gathered. But this also meant that he was always preaching to people on the move; wherefore, it was important that every sermon should proclaim the essential gospel as if for that one time only.[10] This constant itinerancy (both for himself and for his assistants) was of the essence of Wesley's idea of the 'extraordinary ministry'; he never intended to lead a schismatic movement. In 1756 he wrote to Samuel Walker of Truro, 'Were I myself to preach one whole year in one place, I should preach both myself and most of my congregation asleep.'[11] 'The preachers *must* change regularly'; said he to Mrs. Bennis, 'it would never do to let one man sit down for six months with a small society.'[12]

Wesley was by no means the most exciting or eloquent preacher of his time. J. L. von Mosheim, 'the father of modern church history', had not even heard of him in 1755.[13] In Aaron Seymour's dramatic account of the Evangelical Revival Wesley appears as a marginal figure.[14] And yet his influence was cumulative and longer lasting than that of any of the other evangelists of the century. *His* explanation for this, and it is crucial, was that the system of pastoral care and Christian nurture provided for the con-

---

[10] See 'Disciplinary' *Minutes*, June 28, 1744: '*Q*. 13. What is the best general method in preaching? A. (1) To invite. (2) To convince. (3) To offer Christ. Lastly, To build up, and to do this (in some measure) in every sermon.' See also the MS Minutes for May 23, 1753: 'The most effectual way of preaching Christ is to preach him in all his offices, and to declare his law as well as gospel to believers and unbelievers'; and Wesley's open letter, 'Of Preaching Christ', Dec. 20, 1751.

Samplings of Wesley's habit of summarizing the essence of his gospel message in encapsulated form may be seen in Sermons 7, 'The Way to the Kingdom', §I.7-8; 24, 'Sermon on the Mount, IV', §III.1-3; 122, 'The Causes of the Inefficacy of Christianity', §6; and 39, 'Catholic Spirit', §§12-18, etc. Similar summations are scattered through the *Notes* and letters.

[11] Letter, Sept. 3, 1756, to Samuel Walker.

[12] Letter of July 27, 1770; see also his letter to Joseph Benson, Dec. 11, 1772.

[13] See J. S. Reid, *Mosheim's Institutes of Ecclesiastical History* (London, 1849), 873, for a brief notice of Whitefield.

[14] See A. C. H. Seymour, *The Life and Times of Selina, Countess of Huntingdon*, 2 vols. (London, 1840), vol. 1, chs. 12, 14-15; vol. 2, ch. 39. W. Fraser Mitchell, *English Pulpit Oratory* (New York, 1932), 312, ignores Wesley in his list of 'the greatest English preachers'. He was ignored by Erasmus Middleton's survey in his *Evangelical Biography* (London, 1812), and also by John C. Ryle's *Five Christian Leaders of the Eighteenth Century* (London, 1960); Ryle gives John Berridge of Everton a chapter instead.

verts in the 'Methodist connexion' forged them into a mutually sustaining community.[15] He compared the efforts of some of his fellow evangelists among the clergy to 'ropes of sand'.[16] More than anything else, it was Wesley's *message* that struck home: people not excited by his eloquence were moved by his vision of the Christian life and his gospel of universal redemption. This opened the door of hope for men and women who had been crowded off onto the margins of society.[17] Moreover, it was hope in this world as well as in the world to come. Victims of the social and economic dislocations of Hanoverian England had been huddled together on the outskirts of the great cities and around the pitheads of new mines in Cornwall and the North.[18] Wesley had found his new underclass where they were and had gathered them into new social groups in which each person found acceptance and a new sense of dignity. Whitefield and most of the other evangelists found their constituencies largely among the rising middle class and lesser nobility.[19] Thus, if the Church of England was unable to adapt to the new circumstances,[20] Wesley's itinerant system could and did. There is no record of a Methodist society within the bounds of the great cities or their affluent suburbs. But they struck quick root in Moorfields, Spitalfields, Southwark, and similar pockets of poverty around Bristol, Newcastle, and elsewhere.[21] 'I love the poor', said Wesley to Dorothy Furly; 'in many of them I find pure, genuine grace, unmixed with paint, folly, and affectation.'[22] For all the resentment he aroused within

---

[15] See his letter to the 'Travelling Preachers', Aug. 4, 1769, appended to the Annual *Minutes* that year; A *Plain Account of the People called Methodists*, §II.7-10, §VI.1-6 (*Works* 9:262-3, 266-8); and 'Thoughts upon Methodism'; *Arminian Magazine* 10 (1787):100-102, 155-56 (*Works* 9:527-30).

[16] Letter, Aug. 4, 1769; see Sermon 113, *The Late Work of God in North America*, §I.9 and n.

[17] See Christopher Hill, *Society and Puritanism in Pre-Revolutionary England* (London, 1964), 456-57; the 'poor' were excluded from the political process and from most of the protections even of the common law; see also 241, for a comment on the affinities between the Puritans and the rising bourgeoisie.

[18] See George Rudé, 'The Other London' in *Hanoverian London, 1714-1808* (London, 1971), 82-99.

[19] It is true, of course, that Whitefield attracted huge masses to his outdoor services, and he had built a Tabernacle in Moorfields within sight of the Foundery. Even so, his support came largely from the constituency of the Tottenham Court Road Tabernacle and from Lady Huntingdon's Connexion.

[20] See Jonathan Swift's hyperbolic claim that 'five-sixths of the people in England are absolutely hindered from hearing divine service', in *The Prose Works of Jonathan Swift*, ed. Temple Scott, 12 vols. (London, 1897-1925), 1:45. Even so, his point that the churches could not reach beyond their bounds of coterie and custom is valid enough.

[21] See Gay, *Geography*, 146.

[22] Letter of Sept. 25, 1757; see his letter of Sept. 29, 1764, to Ann Foard: '*I bear the rich*

the established churches (Anglican and Nonconformist), the common people heard him gladly and took him to their hearts.

> Outcasts of men, to you I call,
>   Harlots and publicans, and thieves!
> He spreads his arms t'embrace you all;
>   Sinners alone his grace receives:
> No need of him the righteous have,
> He came the lost to seek and save.[23]

The Tradition of Popular Preaching in England

In Wesley's break with eighteenth century taboos against field preaching, extempore prayer, and lay leadership (including his own), he was appealing to larger precedents than those currently being set by men like Howel Harris and George Whitefield. Actually, he was reclaiming a longer, richer tradition that reached back into medieval times and the English Reformation. We have, from G. R. Owst, the fascinating story of the 'lewd' (i.e., popular) preachers and the wandering friars, pardoners, and almoners of the fourteenth and fifteenth centuries.[24] Those men had addressed themselves, as they said, *ad populum* (to the multitude); their messages had ranged from vigorous protests against immorality and injustice to pleas for true compassion and help for the disconsolate poor who had little to hope for from their settled pastors. They, too, had been itinerants, and had 'preached abroad' at the numerous 'preaching crosses' scattered across the land—and not seldom in churchyards and cemeteries.[25] They, too, had been criticized by the generality of bishops and clergy; but they had also found occasional encouragement, as, for example, by so eminent a churchman and scholar as Robert Grosseteste in Wesley's native Lincolnshire.[26] Many of these men were refreshingly free spirits, seeking to re-

---

and love the poor; therefore I spend *almost all* my time with them.' See also his comment in a letter to one of his more sophisticated friends, Brian Bury Collins, Jan. 14, 1780: 'You have seen very little of the choicest part of the London society. I mean the poor. Go with me into their cellars and garrets, and then you will taste their [gracious] spirits.'

[23] 'Where shall my wondering soul begin?' st. 5, in *Hymns and Sacred Poems* (1739), 101–3, No. 29 in Wesley's *Collection of Hymns* (1780), *Works* 7:117.

[24] In his *Preaching in Medieval England* (Cambridge, 1926). See also, E. C. Dargan, *A History of Preaching* (Grand Rapids, 1954), 1:336–42; and R. C. Petry, *No Uncertain Sound* (Philadelphia, 1948), 251–60.

[25] For Wesley's re-enactment of this old populist tradition (*ad populum*), see his Preface to the *Sermons* (*Works* 1:103); for the story about preaching from his father's tombstone in the Epworth churchyard, see *JWJ*, June 6–7, 1742.

[26] Bishop of Lincoln (1235–53), great preacher, reformer, and staunch friend of the

dress the imbalance they saw in their times between the Eucharist and the sermon in Christian worship. Overall, they were also partisans of a Christian puritanism, champions of 'the righteous poore [as] Goddes knyghtes (*patientes pauperes, fideles simplices)*'. They insisted on a radical equality of all persons before God. They denounced pride and avarice as the most pervasive of all the deadly sins, even as they laid great stress on thrift, industry, sobriety, and generosity, as essential Christian virtues.[27] Finally, just as they taught a Christian unworldliness in life, they also taught the Christian 'craft of dying well'.[28] That Wesley stood in their line is clear, and this is important in any interpretation of his self-chosen role as a folk-theologian.

It was inevitable that such a populist tradition would be in disfavour with the establishment at large; after the Lollard ferment, it had been harshly suppressed. At the Reformation, it was partially revived by men like Hugh Latimer and Bernard Gilpin.[29] The same populist tradition, al-

---

Franciscan friars. Matthew Paris's description of him stresses the range of his roles: 'confuter of the pope and the king, . . . preacher to the people (*ad populum)*'; see Henry R. Luard, in *The Dictionary of National Biography*, ed. Sir Leslie Stephen and Sir Sidney Lee, 22 vols. (Oxford, 1921-1923), 'Grosseteste'; henceforth DNB.

[27] See G. R. Owst, *Literature and Pulpit in Medieval England* (Oxford, 1961), 569, 556, 566-68. William Langland's *Piers Plowman's Vision* (c. 1362) may be taken as a kind of distillate of this tradition; see *The Cambridge History of English Literature* (New York, 1933), 2:1-48. Its mysticism and moralism are echoed in Richard Rolle's Northumbrian *Pricke of Conscience* (c. 1430), first published in 1863; see *The Fire of Love* (1435) and *The Mending of Life* (*Cambridge History*, 2:49-54). See also its Kentish predecessor, Dan Michel's tr. of Frère Lorens's *La Somme des vices et vertues* (compiled in 1279), under the title of *The Ayenbite of Inwyt* (1340); see *Cambridge History*, 1:395-96. Chaucer is obviously aware of this tradition, although critical of it, too, as in 'The Wife of Bath, Prologue', and the 'tales' of friar, parson, and pardoner; see Owst, *Literature and Pulpit*, 207-29, 385-97, *et passim*. See the concluding 'tale' ('The Parson's Tale') which turns out to be a *sermon* and, in the end, a kind of 'retraction' of Chaucer's literary enterprise softened by a reaffirmation of the abiding worth of his tr. of Boethius, *De consolatione*. It is worth noting that in the sermon the text (Jer. 6:16 in the Vulgate) is ignored; the discourse is actually about 'Penitence', 'Confession', and 'Satisfaction'. Thus, it amounts to yet another elaboration of the seven deadly sins, with divisions and subdivisions for each heading, and this makes for a striking parallel with *The Ayenbite of Inwyt* and *The Pricke of Conscience*. Clearly, this was a moral and religious tradition that had sunk so deeply into the English conscience that Wesley could take it for granted—as indeed he did. For exhortations to generosity, see Owst, *Literature and Pulpit*, 554-56, with Wesley's 'third rule' for 'The Use of Money'—'Give all you can' (see Sermon 50).

[28] Nancy Lee Beaty, *The Craft of Dying: A Study in the Literary Tradition of the Ars Moriendi in England* (New Haven, 1970), ch. 1, and especially ch. 5 (on Jeremy Taylor). The tradition had come to Wesley most directly from Jeremy Taylor's classic, *The Rule and Exercises of Holy Dying* (1651), *Works* (1844), 1:516-604.

[29] Latimer was a priest of the diocese of Lincoln and licensed in the time of Edward VI to preach 'anywhere in the Kingdom'. He was a vigorous reformer and an obvious target

though with a very different message, had been continued by the early Protestant tractarians, as in, for example, John Frith's widely popular translation of Hamilton's *Places*.[30] During their brief ascendancy in the mid-seventeenth century, the Puritans renewed the tradition yet again by moving their pulpits from the churches to lecture halls and the Parliament.[31] During the Civil War and even after the Restoration, the tradition of 'running lectures' and 'house-creeping ministers' was continued.[32] Meanwhile, the radicals (Quakers, Baptists, Levellers, Ranters, etc.) had also revived the tradition of field preaching without license, to the grave consternation of souls as gentle as that of Richard Baxter.[33] When Whitefield and Wesley took to the fields and to 'itinerating', they were, therefore, renewing an old tradition and giving it new life and power.[34] Even the form of the typical Methodist chapel service reflected a sense of this heritage:

> From the beginning the men and women sat apart, as they always did in the primitive church. And none were suffered to call any place their own, but the first comers sat down first. They had no pews, and all the benches for rich and poor were of the same construction. Mr. Wesley began the service with a short prayer; then sung a hymn and preached (usually about half an hour), then sang a few verses of another hymn, and concluded with prayer. His constant doctrine was salvation by faith, preceded by repentance, and followed by holiness.[35]

---

when Mary Tudor came to the throne; he and Nicholas Ridley were martyred together in Oxford in 1555.

Bernard Gilpin (1517-83) was a popular itinerant and reformer in Elizabeth Tudor's reign (famed as 'the Apostle of the North'). Wesley included an extract of *The Life and Death of Bernard Gilpin* from Samuel Clarke's *Lives of Eminent and Sundry Persons* (1683) in the *Christian Library* 26:99-138, and also again in *Arminian Magazine* 1 (1778):315-25, 363-74, 407-17.

[30] I.e., 'Loci'; Patrick Hamilton (1504?-1528) was Abbot of Dearn, and his *Places: A Treatise on the Law and the Gospel* was translated by John Frith in 1529(?). See also, William A. Clebsch, *England's Earliest Protestants, 1520-1535* (New Haven, 1964), 81-85.

[31] John F. Wilson, *Pulpit in Parliament: Puritanism During the English Civil Wars, 1640-1648* (Princeton, 1969).

[32] See Christopher Hill, *Society and Puritanism*, 80-81; and his *Reformation to Industrial Revolution*, 131.

[33] See John R. H. Moorman, *A History of the Church of England* (London, 1963), ch. 15, 243-48; see also C. E. Whiting, *Studies in English Puritanism* (London, 1931), ch. 6; Hugh Barbour, *The Quakers in Puritan England* (New Haven and London, 1964), chs. 2-3; and *Reliquiae Baxterianae* (1696), Part I, 74-78; note that Baxter's list runs: 'The Vanists—disciples of Sir Henry Vane—The Seekers, The Ranters, The Quakers, and The Behmenists'.

[34] See Horton Davies, *Worship and Theology in England* (Princeton, 1961), 3:202-5.

[35] See 'Thoughts Upon Methodism', §4, *Arminian Magazine* 10 (1787):101 (*Works* 9: 528); see also Wesley's letter to Mary Bishop, Nov. 27, 1770.

'Plain Truth for Plain People'

In his Preface to his very first collection of *Sermons on Several Occasions* (1746) Wesley goes out of his way to stress his commitment to a 'plain style' in preaching.[36] Here again, we have something more than a personal crotchet: it is an echo of a longstanding rivalry between a variety of rhetorical traditions in English preaching that Wesley understood very well and on which he had taken a partisan stand. He knew the tradition of classical learning that had shaped English prose.[37] He understood how eloquence in Greek and Latin depends upon rhythms, sonorities, and images, on neologisms and 'conceits'; he also knew how this had evolved into an 'ornate style' in English preaching, strikingly similar to baroque art and music. The great ones in this latter tradition were Lancelot Andrewes (1555-1626), John Donne (1573-1631), Thomas Playfere (1561?-1609), and Jeremy Taylor (1613-1667). The sermons of Andrewes (Bishop of Ely, Chichester, and, finally, Winchester) are not only richly ornamented; they are intertwinings of intricate prose and poetry, prayer and piety. Donne (Lincoln's Inn and St. Paul's) had delivered and then written out some of the most eloquent sermons in the English language, with rhetorical coruscations as exalted as they are sustained (as in 'Death's Duell', 'The Bells', 'The Church Catholic', etc.). Playfere (a Cambridge professor of divinity) had carried the tradition to excess, a dazzling display of images and conceits where the style often outshines the substance. Jeremy Taylor (Bishop of Down and Connor in Ireland) has more to say than Playfere, but in rhetoric not much less involuted. Over against this there had arisen a plainer, more direct style in the great Edwardian preachers (Thomas Cranmer, John Jewel, Nicholas Ridley)—men who strove for clarity even as they strove to shape their sermons as works of literary art.[38]

It was the Puritans, however, who had elevated the sermon to its place as 'the chief regular means of grace';[39] hence their preference for a centred

---

[36] See Wesley's Preface, §3, in *Works* 1:104: 'I design plain truth for plain people'.

[37] As in Richard Hooker's *Laws of Ecclesiastical Polity* (1594-97), the first great theological treatise by a man who thought in Latin and wrote in English.

[38] See Jewel, *Oratio contra Rhetoricam* (1548), where he decries ornate rhetoric and implies that it was common practice for preachers 'to thrash about with the body, . . . stamp one's feet and to indulge in wild gestures'; see Wilbur Howell, *Eighteenth Century British Logic and Rhetoric* (Princeton, 1971), 123ff. The revival of preaching in the Edwardian prayerbooks and homilies and the eloquence of the prayerbooks themselves, raised the standards of pulpit rhetoric but also contributed to the custom of written sermons to be read to a congregation; the sectaries and the Puritans derided this 'preaching by the book'.

[39] See Davies, *Worship and Theology in England*, 3:31; see also Christopher Hill, *Puritanism and Revolution* (London, 1969), 261-62.

pulpit with its great sounding board and a red velvet cushion for the great pulpit Bible. So also they could speak of preaching as an act of prophecy, as in William Perkins's influential *Art of Prophesying* (1613). *The Order of Prophecy at Norwich. . . .* (1575) was a brief directive to the preachers who would be occupying the pulpit of 'Christ's in Norwich' during the absence of a called and settled pastor. The section of 'prophesying' in *The Directory for the Publique Worship of God* issued by the Westminster Assembly in 1646 reflects this same conception.[40]

The essence of preaching in this tradition was *biblical exposition.* The prophet-preacher's prime task was to find and expound a word from God to his hearers. This freed him from a lectionary but heightened the demand that he choose his texts with the utmost care and then develop them so that no clause or phrase or even word was disregarded. This was implied, as they thought, in the task of 'rightly dividing the word of truth'. This, in its turn, produced some intricate homiletical forms which, in lesser hands, tended toward the ponderous and pedantic 'crumbling of texts' and to elaborations of heads and subheads. Great names in this tradition, after Perkins, were John Owen, Richard Baxter, Stephen Charnock, Isaac Ambrose, Samuel Annesley (Wesley's maternal grandfather), and Isaac Watts (Wesley's older contemporary and something of a rival).

Almost apart from the Anglican-Puritan tensions, the sectaries (Baptists, Quakers, Levellers, etc.) had developed their own tradition of preaching— this one populist and anti-intellectualist. Rejecting 'steeple-houses' and a tax-supported clergy, they took to the fields and meeting-houses, updating, in their way, the older traditions of populist preaching. Their interest in charismatic experiences and their enthusiasm provoked nicknames: Quakers, Ranters, Jumpers. Wesley and the Methodists would, in their turn, face the same sort of ridicule for slightly different reasons.

An alternative to these polarizations had emerged in the seventeenth century, which valued simplicity and clarity above all other homiletical virtues. One may see it in Joseph Mede at Cambridge (who ought to be

---

[40] Perkins's full title is, *The Art of Prophesying; Or, a Treatise Concerning the Sacred and Only True Manner and Method of Preaching,* and the essay appears in Perkins's *Works* (1612-13), 2:646-73; see especially chs. 1, 2 ('The only two duties of the prophet are . . . the preaching of the Word, and praying unto God in the name of the people'), and ch. 3 ('Of the Word of God'). See also William Fulke, *A Brief and Plain Declaration. . . ,* in Leonard Trinterud, ed., *Elizabethan Puritanism,* 256-65 (and Trinterud's comments on the early 'prophesyings' on 191 ff.); see these with the directions on preaching in *The Directory for the Publique Worship of God Throughout the Three Kingdoms of England, Scotland, and Ireland* (1646), 13-18. Much of this lies back of Wesley's description of 'the prophetic ministry' in Sermon 121, 'Prophets and Priests'.

better known for his doctrine of justification than for his millenarian speculations). Its classic expression had been provided by John Wilkins (Bishop of Chester, natural scientist and author of a 'new theory of language') in his *Ecclesiastes: Or, A Discourse Concerning the Gift of Preaching As It Falls Under the Rules of Art* (1679). It was further adapted by Offspring Blackall (Bishop of Exeter) whose *Eighty-Seven Practical Discourses Upon Our Saviour's Sermon on the Mount* (1717-18)[41] served Wesley as a model; and it was reinforced by the essays of James Arderne, *Directions Concerning the Matter and Stile of Sermons* (1671), and Joseph Glanvill, *Essay Concerning Preaching* (1678).

John Wesley knew enough of this background to make his own choice of rhetorical style deliberate. He records reading *The Whole Sermons of that Eloquent Divine of Famous Memory, Thomas Playfere* (1623); if he read them all, he must have been wearied by their 'conceits', which are carried to the edge of caricature. He had also read that charming account in Thomas Fuller of a rhetorical flight in St. Mary's (Oxford) by a 'Mr. Tavernour' in 1558.[42] His reading had included other practitioners of the ornate style of preaching: Richard Sherry, Henry Peacham, Henry Smith, William Chappell—a Puritan—and John Scott.[43] That he knew the Puritans is amply demonstrated in his *Christan Library*[44] and in his Preface to *Sermons 5-8* (1788).[45] But he also deplored their zeal for 'text crumbling'; he understood Robert South's fierce scorn of those so-called 'scribes', whose 'sermons are garnished with quibbles, shreds of Latin and Greek, luxuriant allegories, rhyming cadences . . .'.[46]

Wesley's championship of plain-style preaching had been influenced by

---

[41] These occupied the major part of his *Works*, 2 vols. (1723), 1:1-561, 2:609-939.

[42] See *The Church History of Britain* (1656), Book IX, 65: 'Surely preaching now is very low if it be true what I read [in the Preface to Sir John Cheke's *The True Subject to the Rebell* (1st edition, 1549; rev. edition, 1641)], that Mr. Tavernour, of Water-Eaton in Oxfordshire . . . gave the scholars a sermon in St. Maries . . . beginning with these words: "Arriving at the mount of St. Maries in the stony stage where I now stand [i.e., the high pulpit], I have brought you some fine biskets baked in the oven of charity and carefully conserved for the chickens of the church, the sparrows of the Spirit, and the sweet swallows of salvation."'

[43] See Sherry's Erasmian paraphrase in *A Treatise of Schemes and Tropes* (1550); Peacham, *The Garden of Eloquence* (1577); Henry Smith, *Sermons* (1657); Chappell, *The Preacher: or the Art and Method of Preaching* (1656); John Scott, *Sermons Upon Several Occasions* (1704).

[44] See Robert C. Monk, *John Wesley: His Puritan Heritage* (New York, 1966).

[45] See his references (§5) to 'Dr. [William] Bates, or Mr. John Howe, . . . or Mr. [Jeremiah] Seed'.

[46] See 'The Scribe Instructed', in South's *Sermons Preached Upon Several Occasions* (1st edition, 1737; Philadelphia, 1844), 2:81-85.

his early admiration for his father's plain-style sermons and his discovery in Oxford of the sermons of Benjamin Calamy, William Tilly, and John Tillotson.[47] At Oxford he had read Quintilian's *Institutes*, probably in the great new Burmann edition of 1720. He also read Bartholomew Keckerman's *Rhetoricae Ecclesiasticae* in one of its editions after 1606. But when he decided to furnish his own preachers with a suitable brief manual, he chose an anonymous essay on *The Art of Speaking*,[48] possibly remembered from Oxford; he abridged it under the title, *Directions Concerning Pronunciation and Gesture*.[49] He strove mightily to improve his preachers' pulpit style and general manners,[50] and he deplored excess of any sort. Late in life he would lash out against the superficiality of so-called gospel sermons.[51]

Wesley saw this matter of style as a moral issue; indeed, as a point of national pride. He says as much in the Preface to *Sermons 5–8* (1788): 'I *could* even now write as floridly . . . as even the admired Dr. [Hugh] B[lair].

---

[47] Calamy (1642–1686) had been vicar of London's St. Lawrence Jewry; see his *Sermons Preached Upon Several Occasions* (1687). Tilly was a Fellow of Corpus Christi College, Oxford; M.A., 1697; B.D., 1707; D.D., 1711; see his *Sixteen Sermons . . . Preached Before the University of Oxford Upon Several Occasions* (1712). Tillotson was England's most popular preacher in the generation just before Wesley's; see his *Sermons on Several Occasions* in *Works* (1722). It is interesting that all of these men had the habit of using phrases with paired adjectives (e.g., 'honest and upright'). In abridging their texts Wesley would, almost invariably, strike off one adjective or the other in these pairings.

[48] *The Art of Speaking in Publick: Or an Essay on the Action of an Orator as to His Pronunciation and Gesture* (1727).

[49] Bristol, Farley, 1749.

[50] See the *Minutes* for June 18, 1747, an answer to Q. 11 about 'smaller advices concerning preaching': '(4) Choose the plainest texts you can. (5) Take care not to ramble from your text, but to keep close to it, and make out what you undertake. (6) Always suit your subject to your audience. (7) Beware of allegorizing or spiritualizing too much.' In Wesley's last revision of the Large *Minutes* (1789) there are twenty-one subheads in answer to this question. Note, however, John Hampson's opinion that Wesley's own sermons were not wholly 'superior in elegance' to some of those of his preachers; *Memoirs of the late Rev. John Wesley* (London, 1791), 3:137.

[51] See Sermon 123, 'On Knowing Christ After the Flesh', §11; see also his letter to Mary Bishop, Oct. 18, 1778: 'I myself find more life in the Church prayers than in the formal extemporary prayers of Dissenters. Nay, and I find more profit in sermons on either good tempers or good works than in what are vulgarly called "gospel sermons". That term is now become a mere *cant* word. I wish none of our society would use it. It has no determinate meaning. Let but a pert, self-sufficient animal, that has neither sense nor grace, bawl out something about Christ, or his blood, or justification by faith, and his hearers cry out, "What a fine gospel sermon!" Surely the Methodists have not so learnt Christ. We know no gospel without salvation from sin.' See also Sermon 99, *The Reward of Righteousness*, §I.3, and Wesley's letter to John Broadbent, Feb. 23, 1785: 'Take care you do not *scream* again, unless you would murder yourself outright.'

But I dare not. . . . I dare no more write in a "fine style" than wear a fine coat. . . . I cannot relish French oratory—I despise it from my heart. . . . I am still for plain, sound English.'[52]

There is, therefore, only an apparent irony in Wesley's first Preface (1746), when he ornaments the advertisement of his plain style with two 'shreds of Latin': 'I now write, as I generally speak, *ad populum*, to the bulk of mankind'; and 'Let me be *homo unius libri*' (a man of one book).[53] On first glance, such tags seem out of place. But one would recall how the first phrase, *ad populum*, was not only an echo from an older usage, but also a technical term made recently familiar by yet another great Bishop of Lincoln, Robert Sanderson. In his *Thirty-six Sermons* (1689) Sanderson had distinguished four categories of sermons: (1) *ad aulam* (addresses to a learned audience); (2) *ad magistratum* (sermons on civil occasions to the court or to an assize); (3) *ad clerum* (sermons to clergy); and (4) *ad populum* (sermons to plain people).[54] One should also remember that Wesley *and* his readers would think of such 'shreds' as tokens of a preacher's academic credentials;[55] this is why they were also almost always translated lest a reader be embarrassed or miss the point. Thus, Wesley's tags were not really lapses from his overall claim to plainness. It is a fair guess that such scraps of learning were a sort of reassurance to the Methodists of the superior culture of their leader.

In that same first Preface, Wesley had gone out of his way to stress his intention, in these sermons, 'to forget all that ever I have read in my life'. The only credible meaning for such a disavowal is that he was willing to forego any outward show of learning that might distract his readers. It is obvious that he retained the substance of his reading; his voracious appetite for books of all sorts was never satiated. He read widely all his life, choosing his mentors with care from among the great, near-great, and yet also quite obscure authors whom he 'discovered'. Moreover, he retained a rich concealed deposit of all this for use throughout his life. Thus, as mentor to the Methodists, he digested this material and simplified it to the end that his 'plain people' could hear its 'plain truth' in a rhetoric suited to their needs.

---

[52] See *Works* 2:355-57.

[53] See Preface, §§2, 5, *Works* 1:104-6.

[54] The names of Wesley's father and older brother appear in the 'List of Subscribers' in the front of Sanderson's handsome folio. Thus a copy would have been in the Epworth rectory library, though it probably did not survive the fire of 1709.

[55] See Peter Gay, *The Enlightenment: An Interpretation*, vol. 1: *The Rise of Modern Paganism* (New York, 1966), 119.

He wore his learning so lightly that many have been deceived thereby. His quotations and allusions are careless (although rarely misleading); his abridgements are invariably biased, and yet often very deft. His *Christian Library* is an anthology culled from a huge bibliography, reduced by a ratio of roughly one page to fifty. The bulk of his 'sources' were Puritans (in one or another sense of that indefinable term), but 'predestination' had been carefully screened out of their treatises, to adapt them to what Wesley judged was their edifying core of common Christian piety.[56] His *Extract of Mr. Richard Baxter's Aphorisms of Justification* (1745) is an instructive example of Wesley's way with sources. Baxter had published the *Aphorisms* in 1649, but had quickly thereafter disavowed them as a misleading statement of his actual views. Thus there were no further editions of the *Aphorisms* after 1649; in their place Baxter had composed a *Confession of Faith* (1655), with the same doctrine of divine initiative and human response more carefully nuanced. Wesley discovered a copy of the original *Aphorisms* in 1745, a rare book then, and rarer since. Preferring the *Aphorisms* over the *Confession*, Wesley 'extracted' them for the use of his preachers and people, blithely ignoring Baxter's disavowals.[57] In his *Extract* Wesley discarded all of Baxter's copious technical references, along with the careful distinction between God's 'decretive' and 'elective' will; Baxter's eighty 'theses' were reduced to Wesley's forty-five 'propositions'.

Two further examples of Wesley's habit of editing obscure texts according to his special purposes may be worth noting here; both appear in the *Arminian Magazine*. The first is a highly condensed extract from an important book by an obscure author, one John Plaifere: *Appello Evangelium* (1651). Plaifere is missing from the *Dictionary of National Biography*, and there are only six copies of his only book listed in the *National Union*

---

[56] In 1772 Sir Richard Hill denounced Wesley in *A Review of All the Doctrines Taught by the Rev. Mr. John Wesley*; he was particularly incensed by Wesley's editorial biases, and asked, 'Why must poor John Bunyan be disembowelled to make him look like Mr. Wesley?' Wesley's bland reply in *Some Remarks on Mr. Hill's Review*, §12.(34), is that Bunyan's Calvinism had been omitted 'to make him like the authors going before him. . . . However, those that are fond of his bowels may put them in again and swallow them as they would the train of a woodcock.' Earlier, in §12.(1), he had explained that he had not proofread *A Christian Library*, and blamed 'the correctors of the press', 'through whose inattention an hundred passages were left in which I had scratched out'.

[57] None of his readers would have known anything about this history of the *Aphorisms*; Wesley knew it from Baxter's own comments in *Reliquiae Baxterianae*, Part I, 107-8, 111. He also knew and 'extracted' Baxter's *Call to the Unconverted* (1658) in 1782. There is no recorded evidence of his having read Baxter's *Confession of Faith*, but more than once he recommended Baxter, e.g., his letters to Richard Locke, Sept. 14, 1770, and to Thomas Davenport, Dec. 23, 1782.

Catalog, Pre–1956 Imprints. It is merely typical that Wesley took an elaborate text of four hundred and thirty-five octavo pages and reduced it to less than seventy; what is significant is that, in the process, the longest passage that remains almost intact is a brief discussion of justification from the so-called 'King's Book' of 1543 (*A Necessary Doctrine and Erudition for Any Christian Man*), a passage contributed by Stephen Gardiner.[58] Wesley may or may not have known Plaifere's source for this quotation. What matters is that he found the passage worth retaining.

Still another sampling from Wesley's extraordinary repertoire (and a good example of how he put his learning to unobtrusive use) is an English translation of Sebastian Castellio's dialogues on predestination, election, freewill, and faith.[59] Wesley had found them bound together with Castellio's elegant Ciceronian translation of à Kempis's *De Imitatione Christi* from its rude Latin original; this he wanted for his students at Kingswood School. But he also decided that Castellio's dialogues would be edifying for his people, and so he prepared an English translation for publication in the volumes of the *Arminian Magazine* for 1781 and 1782. It is a very good translation, too, and the only one in English that these dialogues have ever had; it still remains ignored by Castellio scholars.[60] Wesley's prefatory note is quietly understated:

> Numberless treatises have been written in this and the last age on the subject of predestination; but I have not seen any that is written with more good sense and good humour than Castellio's *Dialogues*, wrote above two hundred years ago. Yet I know not that they have ever appeared in our tongue. I believe therefore the putting them into an English dress will give pleasure to every impartial reader.[61]

Wesley's stake in this sort of learning and his 'concealment' of it came from his passion for a message that would gather into itself the riches of both Christian and classical traditions and that still could be shared with his 'plain people'. This is what lies behind and beneath the surface rhet-

---

[58] Catholic bishop of London until exiled by Edward VI; he was recalled by Mary Tudor as Bishop of Winchester; there he married the beleaguered queen to Prince Philip of Spain in 1554; see Carolly Erickson, *Bloody Mary* (Garden City, N.Y., 1978), 373ff.

[59] *Dialogi IIII. De praedestinatione, De electione, De libero arbitrio, De fide* (Gouda, 1578). This 1st edition had been interdicted by Queen Elizabeth's advisers; the dialogues were never published in England.

[60] There is no reference to Wesley's translation in any of the Castellio literature that I have seen; see Ferdinand Buisson, *Sébastien Castellion: sa Vie et son Oeuvre, 1515–1563*, (Paris, 1964), *Appendice, Piéces Inédites*, cxviii, 2:498–99.

[61] *Arminian Magazine* 4 (1781):vi.

oric of the sermons, including his claim to be *homo unius libri*. It is this veiled background which, nevertheless, gives the sermons themselves an extra dimension of depth and originality rarely found in typical popularizers.[62] By and large, such men work within cultural limitations and with even less care for the Christian tradition as a whole. Their strength has usually come from their fluency with Scripture and their confident self-reliance on personal experience and charisma. The great exceptions are quite different: geniuses who are great theologians and popular preachers both in one. Luther comes to mind,[63] or St. Chrysostom,[64] or even St. Augustine *in his sermons*.[65] No claim could ever be made that Wesley's talents ranked him in such a company. And yet, the analogy of effective preachers preaching out of a rich overflow is not amiss, and it is only fair to see Wesley apart from the generality of popularizers. These sermons in their contexts may, therefore, help to exhibit Wesley as the special sort of theologian that he was; and such an exhibition might further suggest that his theology deserves more serious consideration than it has yet had from historians of Christian thought in general.

---

[62] See William Perkins, *The Art of Prophesying*, in his *Works*, vol. 2, ch. x: 'In the promulgation [of a sermon] two things are required: the hiding of human wisdom and the demonstration or showing of the Spirit. . . . Human wisdom must be concealed whether it be in the matter of the sermon or in the setting forth of the words, because the testimony of the Word is the testimony of God, and the profession of the knowledge of Christ and not of human skill: and again because the hearers ought not to ascribe their faith to the gifts of men but to the power of God's Word. . . . If any man thinketh that by this means barbarism should be brought into pulpits, he must understand that the minister may, yea and must privately, use at his liberty the arts, philosophy, and a variety of reading whilst he is inframing his sermon, but he ought in public to conceal all these from the people and not to make the least ostentation.' See also p. 56, n. 35 below.

[63] See *The Liberty of a Christian Man*, §1; see also his *Catechisms* addressed to children, still grist for professional theologians.

[64] See W. R. W. Stephens, *Saint John Chrysostom; . . . A Sketch of the Church and Empire in the Fourth Century*, 2nd edition (London, 1880), 422, 426ff. See also Stephens's editing of Chrysostom's treatises and homilies in *Nicene and Post-Nicene Fathers, II*, (New York, 1890–1900), vol. 9.

[65] As in Sister Sarah Muldowney, R.S.M., *St. Augustine: Sermons on the Liturgical Seasons*, in *Fathers of the Church* (New York, 1959), and in Quincy Howe, Jr., *Selected Sermons of St. Augustine* (New York, 1966); see especially Howe's 'Introduction'.

3. THE SERMON CORPUS

The Early Sermons

Conventional wisdom among Wesley biographers is to the effect that, during his Oxford years, he was something of a recluse and an 'enthusiast'.[1] They have ignored the fact that the young Mr. Wesley was actually a more popular preacher than most of his colleagues; his record of preaching in and around Oxford, in Christ Church Cathedral and St. Mary's, in the decade between his ordination as deacon (Sept. 19, 1725) and his departure for Georgia (Oct. 21, 1735) suggests a man of parts and of general acceptance as well. In that one decade he wrote some sixty-eight sermons of his own, and he preached many of them more than once.[2] He also 'collected' a full notebook of sermons from other authors and preached these to various audiences, too (e.g., in the Oxford prisons).[3] These sermons are important, therefore, as reflections of Wesley's early views and as portents of his later developments. But for the most part they are unimpressive as sermons, and so have been all too easily ignored by most students of Wesley's thought.

The reasons for this are obvious: they simply do not fit the conventional Methodist stereotypes or the stereotypes of others about Wesley. Wesley's tacit acknowledgement of their mediocrity is suggested by the fact that he

---

[1] See Richard Watson, *The Life of the Rev. John Wesley* (New York and London, 1831), ch. 2; Tyerman, *John Wesley* 1:66–71; even Southey, *Wesley*, ch. 2. Wesley had given credence to this image in his *JWJ* retrospective for May 24, 1738 (§§4–7): 'Removing soon after to another college, I executed a resolution which I was before convinced was of the utmost importance, shaking off at once all my trifling acquaintance. . . . I abridged myself of all superfluities. . . . I soon became "a byword" for so doing.'

[2] Most of what we know of these early sermons and their sequence comes from the pioneering work of Richard P. Heitzenrater and his decipherings of Wesley's Oxford Diaries; see his 'John Wesley's Early Sermons', in *WHS* 37 (1970):110–28, and also his unpublished dissertation, 'John Wesley and the Oxford Methodists, 1725–35' (Duke University, 1972). Heitzenrater's decipherment and transcription of Wesley's 1735–41 Diaries are in *Works* 18:299–577, and 19:353–474. The Oxford Diaries will be published in vol. 32 of *Works*. His work supersedes Curnock's and Green's and provides us, for the first time, with adequate data for a detailed study of Wesley's day-to-day life and work. My narrative here is greatly indebted to Heitzenrater's findings.

[3] See vol. 19 in the Colman Collection, Methodist Archives, The John Rylands University Library of Manchester.

included only one of them (lightly revised) in his later collection of *Sermons on Several Occasions*, Volumes 1–4.[4] Nor does he tell us how far some of them may have served him as 'first drafts' for later sermons on the same texts in the *Arminian Magazine* and *Sermons*, Volumes 5–8. Eighteen of these manuscript sermons have survived, and also two fragments. Of these, Joseph Benson published four,[5] along with three others mistakenly attributed to Wesley.[6] Thomas Jackson followed Benson's order generally but added another manuscript sermon, on Isa. 1:21, which he entitled, 'True Christianity Defended'.[7] He also felt bound to warn his readers that

> these discourses, it will be observed, were written before Mr. Wesley obtained correct views of the way of salvation; and as they were not published either with his knowledge or appointment, he should not be made responsible for the sentiments which they contain.[8]

Jackson also added Wesley's first published sermon, on Job 3:17, to which he assigned a title, 'The Trouble and Rest of Good Men'.[9]

A legend soon sprang up based on a misleading *Journal* entry from October 16, 1771, that Wesley's first venture into a pulpit had been in the parish church of South Leigh on Sunday, September 26, 1725, with his text from Matt. 6:33.[10] In 1903 a crude transcript of this sermon was published in pamphlet form (in London) entitled, 'Wesley's First Sermon'. Professor Heitzenrater, however, has identified 'a listing of John Wesley's

---

[4] See Sermon 17, 'The Circumcision of the Heart'; Sermon 48, 'Self-denial,' is from the same text as one of the Oxford sermons.

[5] (1) A funeral sermon of Jan. 11, 1727, but not at Epworth, *pace* Benson (on 2 Sam. 12:33; see Sermon 136); (2) an Epworth sermon, 'On Corrupting the Word of God', of Oct. 6, 1727, on 2 Cor. 2:17 (see Sermon 137); (3) his inaugural sermon in Savannah, Feb. 20, 1736, 'On Love', on 1 Cor. 13:3 (see Sermon 149); and (4) another Epworth sermon of Sept. 3, 1732, from Amos 3:6 (see Sermon 143); this latter is in John's hand and is based on an incident recorded in his diary, but it reads more like it might have been preached by his father and copied out by John.

[6] (1) 'On the Resurrection of the Dead' (1 Cor. 15:35), from Benjamin Calamy, *Sermons*, 11 (published by Wesley in the *Christian Library* 39:246–73; see *Works* 4:528–30, (2) 'On Grieving the Holy Spirit' (Eph. 4:30), from William Tilly, *Sermons*, 11 (published in *Methodist Magazine* 21 (1798):607–13, as 'an original sermon of Mr. Wesley's'; see *Works* 4:531); and (3) a university sermon of June 13, 1736, 'On the Holy Spirit' (2 Cor. 3:17) by John Gambold, and in John Gambold's handwriting (see *Works* 4:524).

[7] This was Wesley's own composition, in two versions (Lat. and Eng.); see Sermons 150 and 151, 'Hypocrisy in Oxford'.

[8] Jackson's prefatory note to his 'Fifth Series' of sermons in *Works* (Jackson), 7:451.

[9] Wesley had preached this in St. Mary's on Sept. 21, 1735, and Charles Rivington had published it in November. See Thomas Jackson's disparaging estimate of it in his edition; *Works* (Jackson), 7:365.

[10] See Curnock's imagined reconstruction of this event in his edition of the *JWJ*, 1:60.

early sermons numbered *in the order that he wrote them'* on the verso, 'opposite a page [of the first Oxford diary] dated 24th September 1726'.[11] From this list and its enumerations it would appear that Wesley's very first sermon had been preached most probably in the church at Fleet Marston (from Job 3:17) and probably on October 3, 1725; which is to say, a bare fortnight after his diaconal ordination.[12] There are entries on this manuscript that indicate a repetition of the same sermon more than ten times during the next sixteen months in other small churches in the vicinity, including South Leigh (Feb. 12, 1727).[13] The sermon on Matt. 6:33 was his second sermon; it was written in November of 1725 and preached at several places noted on the manuscript: 'Buckland, Stanton, Wroot, Broadway, Binsey', etc. The next holograph in this sequence is a funeral sermon for a close friend, Robin Griffiths, preached in the parish church of Broadway on January 15, 1727. It is Wesley's first sermon with an idea somewhat out of the ordinary: *viz.*, that bodily death amounts to a conquest of sin which has its seat in the flesh; hence, Christians need not mourn unduly for their loved ones who have died in the faith.[14] The fourth surviving sermon from this sequence (Sermon 137, 'On Corrupting the Word of God') was written while Wesley was assisting his father in Epworth and Wroot in 1728–29; one thinks it may have been an oblique tribute to his father's stubborn integrity and faithfulness in interpreting the Bible to his obdurate parishioners. It is interesting that Wesley preserved this manuscript in his papers for more than sixty years; a slightly revised version of it was published posthumously in *The Methodist Magazine* in 1798. Yet another manuscript surviving from those Epworth days is dated January 17, 1728;[15] this is not the same sermon that appeared much later in the *Arminian Magazine* (1785), and in *Sermons* 7 (1788), even though their Scripture texts are identical.[16] We know of a sermon on Gen. 3:19 that was written in Epworth in 1728; a sermon on the same text was later published

---

[11] 'John Wesley's Early Sermons', p. 111.

[12] The holograph of this sermon is in the Morley Collection of Wesleyana in Wesley College, Bristol (Sermon 133), along with 'On Dissimulation' (Sermon 138A) and the Latin text of 'Hypocrisy in Oxford' (Sermon 151).

[13] It was in *this* sense that he preached 'his first sermon at South Leigh'.

[14] An echo of a doctrine that runs back at least to the *Apology of the Augsburg Confession* (1531), Art. XII, §§151–61, as, e.g., 'Death itself serves this same [positive] purpose: to destroy this sinful flesh so that we may rise completely renewed' (§153); see T. G. Tappert, ed., *The Book of Concord* (Philadelphia, 1959), 206–8. See also Heinrich Schmid, *Doctrinal Theology of the Evangelical Lutheran Church*, 2nd english edition, rev. (Philadelphia, 1899), 263, 624.

[15] See Sermon 138A, 'On Dissimulation'.

[16] See Sermon 90, 'An Israelite Indeed'.

in the *Arminian Magazine* (1782), and in *Sermons* 5 (1788). Still another sermon (on Matt. 26:26) was written in 1728; it may have been a prototext for Sermon 84, *The Important Question*, which was first published in 1775 and then included in *Sermons* 7 (1788). This may also have been the case with his first sermon on Luke 9:23 and his later Sermon 48, 'Self-denial'. We know of an undated sermon on Ps. 8:4 that may still have been in Wesley's papers when he wrote the sermon that appeared in the *Arminian Magazine* in 1788 and was later reprinted in the posthumous *Sermons* 9 (1800). Another Epworth sermon of late 1728 or early 1729 was based on Rom. 11:33; Sermon 68, 'The Wisdom of God's Counsels', published in the *Arminian Magazine* in 1784 and in *Sermons* 6 (1788), has the same text. Similar duplication of texts, from the Epworth period to the time of the later Wesley, may be seen in the case of a sermon on Eph. 5:16 (see Sermon 93, 'On Redeeming the Time'), and a sermon recorded in Wesley's diary list prior to August, 1729; also a sermon on Luke 12:7.[17]

One reason for this conjecture that Wesley's early sermons may have been prototexts for his later ones is simply that they have not survived; all the manuscripts of the sermons that Wesley published seem to have been discarded by his printers. Thus the holographs in his papers at his death must have been pieces that he had cherished, and, presumably, had put to some use or other instead of handing them over to a printer.

At any rate, he returned to Oxford in late November of 1729 at the behest of his rector, John Morley, to resume his duties there. He continued to write sermons and preach them in nearby churches, and also, presently, in the prisons. What would seem to have been his first 'university sermon' was produced in late October, and preached in St. Mary's on November 15, 1730. Its text is Gen. 1:27, and it is easily Wesley's most interesting and original effort up to that date. His earlier sermons do not prepare his readers for the new flights of speculation here about Adam's perfections ('the image of God') or the tragic consequences of Adam's fall (including bodily weaknesses, one of which sounds very much like atherosclerosis). After fifty mediocre sermons, here is finally one with a touch of genius;[18] Wesley preached it at least four times more (in London, at Stanton, again in London, and in St. Miles', in Oxford). In September, 1731, Wesley wrote a sermon on Mark 9:48 which has not survived; a sermon on the same text appeared in the *Arminian Magazine* in 1782, but it would have

---

[17] The sermon on this text is dated in the fortnight of Aug. 7-22, 1729, when Wesley was back in Oxford for a visit; the published sermon on Luke 12:17, 'On Divine Providence' (Sermon 67), appeared first in the *Arminian Magazine* 9 (1786):125-32, 185-93.

[18] See Sermon 141, 'The Image of God'.

had to have been written after 1759, since one of its most striking illustrations has to do with an asbestos handkerchief that Wesley had seen in the 'new' British Museum, not opened to the public till 1759.

The most outstanding of these early sermons—destined to stand as a landmark in Wesley's entire theological development thereafter—was his second 'university sermon', preached in St. Mary's, January 1, 1733.[19] His diaries record the fact that he spent the better part of a month preparing his manuscript; what they do not explain is its marked advance beyond any of Wesley's previous statements of his vision of the holy life. In it, all that he had learned from Taylor, à Kempis, William Law, and the traditions of Christian will-mysticism behind them comes to focus. It provides the earliest summing up of what would thereafter be the essence of his doctrine of grace. That he realized later how nearly successful he had been is suggested by his careful placement of it in a slightly revised version at the head of his second volume of *Sermons* (1748), which is also to say, as the first in the series of his sermons on holy living as the fruit of justifying faith. As an old man, he would confirm this earlier judgment: 'I know not that I can [even now] write a better [sermon] on "The Circumcision of the Heart" than I did five-and-forty years ago.'[20]

One of Professor Heitzenrater's more unexpected discoveries is that nine of John Wesley's early sermons have survived through the undesigned good offices of his brother Charles.[21] The evidence for this comes from the volume of thirteen sermons in Charles's handwriting in the Methodist Archives; eleven of these, heavily edited, were published posthumously in *Sermons by the Late Rev. Charles Wesley, A.M.* (1816). From the shorthand notes on the manuscripts, and from other references, Heitzenrater has concluded that Charles, newly ordained just before the Georgia mission, had borrowed and transcribed some of John's manuscript sermons, 'at various times during Charles' excursion to America in 1735-36'. One of these (on Ps. 91:11) would date back as early as September, 1726.[22] Another ('On the Sabbath') had been written in July of 1730 and preached twelve times between July 19, 1730 and September 9, 1733. The sermon of his brother's that Charles seems to have liked best (as far as we can tell from his own *Journal*) was the one on Luke 10:42.[23]

---

[19] See Sermon 17, 'The Circumcision of the Heart'.

[20] JWJ, Sept. 1, 1778.

[21] Heitzenrater, 112-13; see also his chart on 116-27.

[22] And this would mean that Sermon 135, 'On Guardian Angels', would be one of the earliest in the entire sermon corpus.

[23] See Sermon 146, 'The One Thing Needful', which had, in its turn, been based on

Besides these sermons that have survived either in John's handwriting or in Charles's transcriptions, there are eight other manuscripts also in John's hand that he had 'collected' and used in his preaching as occasions seemed to warrant.[24] The significance for us of such borrowings is their indication of Wesley's instinctive dependence upon typical Anglican authors for his doctrine of holy living.[25] They also remind us that at this stage of his career Wesley felt no special need to establish himself as an original preacher in his own right: this practice of adapting and using material from others was a commonplace in his time.

These early sermons have been neglected by Wesley's disciples chiefly on the grounds of their doctrine; others have found them scarcely worth the trouble of serious analysis; others have never even noticed them at all.[26] And there is no denying that even in an age of perfunctory preaching they are generally unmemorable. This fact sheds some light on another one: that, for all of Wesley's zeal in that first decade, his early preaching was largely ineffectual.[27]

And yet they contain many a seed of Wesley's later, mature ideas. His conception of the essence of 'holiness' as love of God and neighbour is there, along with his view of sanctification as more of a process than a state. There is also his platonizing theory of religious knowledge as more intuitive than discursive, along with his distinctive sense of the personal, prevenient action of the Holy Spirit in all authentic spirituality. These sermons reflect a version of the ascetical-mystical tradition in English Christianity, and its succession from the medieval mystics (and moralists) down to his father's friend, John Norris, and to his own mother. Here is the source of a conviction that never left him: that holiness and true happiness are correlates, and this by God's specific design.[28] Behind his identified sources (Taylor,

---

Jeremy Taylor's *Unum Necessarium: Or, the Doctrine and Practice of Repentance* (1655).

[24] See *Works* 4:525.

[25] There is a special case with respect to Sermon 101, 'The Duty of Constant Communion'. As it stands, it is enough of Wesley's own work to be printed with his *Sermons*; its substance, however, is greatly indebted to an earlier essay of Robert Nelson on *The Great Duty of Frequenting the Christian Sacrifice* (1707); see *Works* 4:526-28.

[26] As, e.g., Martin Schmidt.

[27] See *The Principles of a Methodist Farther Explained*, §VI.1: 'From the year 1725 to 1729 I preached much, but saw no fruit of my labour; . . . from 1734 to 1738, speaking more of faith in Christ, I saw more fruit of my preaching . . . than ever I had done before; . . . from 1738 to this time, speaking continually of Jesus Christ, . . . the "Word of God ran" as fire among the stubble.'

[28] See Sermon 5, 'Justification by Faith', §I.4 and n.; in no less than thirty of his sermons Wesley rings the changes on the theme: *only the holy can ever be truly happy*. See Franklin L. Baumer's comment that 'happiness was the universal obsession of the age', in

à Kempis, Law) there loomed a great cloud of witnesses whose names we
have to glean elsewhere (Henry Scougal, Lorenzo Scupoli [Juan de Cas-
tañiza], John Cardinal Bona, Gaston de Renty, Gregory Lopez, and many
another).[29] And behind this Latin tradition lay the balancing, deepening
influence of Greek Catholic spirituality (with its distinctive pneumatology
that Wesley embraced wholeheartedly), with roots that run from Ignatius of
Antioch through Irenaeus and Clement of Alexandria, to Macarius, Gregory of Nyssa, Ephrem Syrus, and the great Eastern liturgies.[30]

On its other side this same Anglican tradition reflected in these early
sermons includes a radical emphasis on human freedom and responsibility.
Men, it seems to say, *can* live blamelessly if they so choose and, therefore,
ought to—although for all venial lapses the church has an ample store of
'the means of grace' on which the repentant faithful may rely for 'pardon
and amendment of life'. Calvinists lumped all such views under their epi-
thet, 'Arminian', and included Wesley, too. But the young Wesley had
never read Arminius, as far as we know;[31] he had inherited this part of
his tradition from men like William Laud, Charles Hickman, John Hinton,
Browne Willis, and still more recently, George Bull, Peter Heylyn, Benjamin Hoadly, and John Tillotson.[32] There is no sign that he was ever

---

Modern European Thought; Continuity and Change in Ideas, 1600–1950 (New York, 1977),
142; see also Paul Hazard, *La Pensée Européenne au XVIII Siècle* (Paris, 1946), vol. 1, ch. 2;
and Robert Mauzi, *L'Idée du bonheur.* . . . (Paris, 1960).

[29] See Jean Orcibal, 'Les Spirituels Francais et Espagnols chez John Wesley et ses con-
temporains', in *Revue d'Histoire des Religions* (1951), 139:50-109, and 'The Theological
Originality of John Wesley and Continental Spirituality', in Rupert Davies and Gordon
Rupp, eds., *A History of the Methodist Church in Great Britain* (London, 1965), 1:83-111;
also Robert G. Tuttle, Jr., *John Wesley: His Life and Theology* (Grand Rapids, 1978), 217-27.

[30] See Albert C. Outler, ed., *John Wesley*, in A Library of Protestant Thought (New York,
1964), 9, 12-13, 31, 119. For Wesley's chief early source in the ancient liturgies, see William Beveridge's massive *Synodikon, Sive Pandectae Canonum SS. Apostolorum, et Conciliorum
ab Ecclesia Graeca Receptorum* (1672), 2 vols.

[31] Frank Baker doubts if he ever read much of Arminius's own writings; see WHS 22
(1940):118-19. The fact that he was labelled 'Arminian' is no proof of his direct dependence upon Arminius himself.

[32] William Laud, Archbishop of Canterbury, 1633-45; see Edward C. E. Bourne, *The
Anglicanism of William Laud* (London, 1947). Charles Hickman, Bishop of Derry, 1703-13;
see *The Christian Faith Explain'd and Vindicated.* . . . (1713), in *Twelve Sermons Preached at
St. James's, Westminster* (1713). John Hinton, Prebendary of Sarum; see *A Sermon . . . on the
Day of Thanksgiving for His Majesty's late Victory over the* [Monmouth] *Rebels* (1685). Browne
Willis (1682-1760) was the anonymous author of a new treatise on *The Whole Duty of Man,
Abridged for the Benefit of the Poorer Sort* (1717). Wesley refers to this in his Preface to his
abridgment of [Richard Allestree?], *The Whole Duty of Man* (1657) in the *Christian Library*,
vol. 13 (1753): '. . . the ensuing tract [i.e., of 1657] far better deserves its title than that mis-
erable thing which has lately usurped the name' [i.e., Willis's version]. Seth Ward (1617-

tempted to the deistic tendencies of this tradition.[33]

Likewise, there is no discernible evidence in these early sermons of any acquaintance with 'England's earliest Protestants'—Robert Barnes, Patrick Hamilton, Simon Fish, and others.[34] Nor can it be proved, *from the sermons*, that he knew the great Puritans (William Perkins, William Ames, John Bunyan), or even the Lambeth Articles of 1595.[35] This makes it all the more interesting that as early as 1739 he could write and publish a sermon against George Whitefield's Calvinism that reflects a competent knowledge of the Puritan cause and, in the same year, publish an 'extract' of *Two Treatises*. . . . of Robert Barnes, the Dominican friar turned Lutheran, who had been burned by Henry VIII.[36] And since he could scarcely have discovered Barnes and Perkins and the others in the months after Aldersgate, this suggests that his theological orientation at Oxford had been very much more complete than he would afterward report.

In any case, there is a drastic contrast between these early sermons and the later ones, in substance, verve, and spirit. And this poses one of the most interesting problems in Wesley studies: the metamorphosis of an ineffectual zealot into an effectual evangelist, the sudden growth of a pur-

---

1689), successively Bishop of Exeter and Salisbury; see *Seven Sermons* (1674). For Hoadly and Tillotson, see Irène Simon, 'Anglican Rationalism in the Seventeenth Century', ch. 2 in *Three Restoration Divines* (Paris, 1967); see also H. R. McAdoo, *The Structure of Caroline Moral Theology* (London and New York, 1949), and E. C. Mossner, *Bishop Butler and the Age of Reason* (New York, 1936), especially ch. 1.

[33] The deists he knew best were Matthew Tindal (see his *Rights of the Christian Church asserted against the Romish and all other Priests who claim an Independent Power Over It*, 1706, and *Christianity as Old as the Creation*, 1730); Anthony Collins (see his *Essay Concerning the Use of Reason*, 1707, and *A Discourse of Freethinking*, 1713); and Anthony Ashley Cooper, Third Earl of Shaftesbury (*Characteristicks of Men, Manners, Opinions, Times*, 1711). His best known rationalists, by far, were John Locke (*The Reasonableness of Christianity*, 1695) and Samuel Clarke (*The Evidences of Natural and Revealed Religion*, 1706).

[34] So convincingly 'recovered' by Clebsch in *England's Earliest Protestants*.

[35] William Perkins (1558-1602); see his *Armilla Aurea* (1590, 1592); Eng. tr., *A Golden Chaine; Or the Description of Theology, Containing the Causes of Salvation and Damnation, According to God's Word* (1591; 2nd edition, much enlarged, 1597; 3rd edition, 1600). William Ames (1576-1633), a student of Perkins at Cambridge; see his *Medulla S. S. Theologiae* (1629); Eng. version, *The Marrow of Sacred Divinity* (1642). See Bunyan's *The Doctrine of Law and Grace Unfolded* (1659), *A Defence of the Doctrine of Justification by Faith in Christ* (1672), and *Reprobation Asserted* (1674?).

[36] See Barnes, *Two Treatises. The First, On Justification by Faith Only*. . . . *The Second, On the Sinfulness of Man's Natural Will*. The original is from *The Workes of Doctour Barnes* [together with 'The Whole Workes' of W. Tyndale, John Frith, etc.] (1573). Wesley's extract is from Part 4 of Barnes's text, entitled, 'Faith onely justifieth before God' (pp. 226-27); Barnes's second treatise is entitled, 'Freewill of Man, after the fall of Adam, of his natural strength, can he nothyng but sinne afore God' (pp. 267-68).

veyor of commonplaces into a folk-theologian whose influence would be perduring. It goes without saying, however, that all simplistic explanations of this metamorphosis are just that.

Sermons on Several Occasions, *Volumes 1–4*

During the summer of 1746 Wesley interrupted his itinerant schedule for several weeks in order to prepare a slight volume of sermons for publication—the first of three designed to exhibit 'the substance of what I have been preaching for between eight and nine years last past'. It was his hope that 'every serious man who peruses these [might] see, in the clearest manner, what these doctrines are which I embrace and teach as the essentials of true religion'.[37]

That phrase, 'for between eight and nine years last past', points to a self-conscious and radical shift in Wesley's understanding of the priorities in the order of salvation; it also reflects a radical new turn that his career had taken since 1738. Its vagueness ('between eight and nine years') implies that his evangelical conversion was not to be tied to any one single event, but rather to a series of them that had run throughout that year, beginning with his deep depression in the wake of his Georgia fiasco.[38] The essence of the shift had been a reversal of his earlier view that holy living is in order to justifying faith into an evangelical conviction that justifying faith is in order to holy living. This change had not come easily. He had been challenged to it by the Moravians and Salzburgers in Georgia.[39] The turmoil had then been intensified in a protracted dialogue between Wesley and Peter Böhler, a Moravian missionary who happened to be in England in transit to America. Wesley had met Böhler on February 7, 1738, and the two were nearly constant companions till the latter's departure on May 8.[40] The dialogue had borne its fruits in Wesley's climactic experience of *personal assurance* in an Anglican-Moravian society in Aldersgate Street in the evening of May 24 when, during the reading of 'Luther's preface to the

---

[37] Preface, §1, *Works* 1:103.

[38] Reported in two vivid memoranda, the first in *JWJ*, Jan. 8–9, 1738; and a 'Second Paper' of Jan. 25; see *Works* 18:212–13. Together, these constitute one of Wesley's more important theological self-revelations.

[39] One of Martin Schmidt's more important contributions in this area was his demonstration of the special influence of the Salzburgers along with the Moravians in preparing Wesley for his 'new' gospel. See his essay, 'Wesley's Place in Church History', in Kenneth E. Rowe, ed., *The Place of Wesley in the Christian Tradition* (Metuchen, N. J., 1976), 67–93.

[40] See also Böhler's 'last word' in the debate, in his letter to Wesley from the dockside in Southampton; Wesley printed it in *JWJ*, May 10, 1738.

Epistle to the Romans', he had suddenly 'felt [his] heart strangely warmed.'[41] He had then promptly declared his new-found faith in faith at St. George's, Bloomsbury, on the following Sunday, at Stanton Harcourt a fortnight later (June 11), and in a sermon to the university on that same afternoon.[42]

Wesley spent the following summer in Germany with the Moravians at Herrnhut and Marienborn, where his confidence in the doctrine of faith alone had been strengthened and his personal attachment to the Moravians weakened. Still another crisis followed in October with his discovery of Jonathan Edwards's newly published *Faithful Narrative*, with its details about an actual revival being stirred by a pietism very like his own, even though he himself was still 'beating the air'.[43] What is most significant here is that these cumulative challenges drove him back, as if by instinct, to his own Anglican roots. There, in the *Homilies*, he had finally found the theological font of his own heritage; this doctrine of justification remained as a fixed benchmark for the rest of his theological development.[44]

He had now settled his soteriology in what would be its stable order thenceforth; he had experienced for himself the assurance of grace;[45] and yet his preaching was still comparatively fruitless. This had changed abruptly in April of 1739 when, with grim distaste, he had ventured into the fields near Bristol and had found an unexpectedly positive response. This, in effect, had confirmed his own faith, and had launched his new career as an evangelist—the spiritual director of a revival movement that was to take on a life of its own, sweeping Wesley along with its progress as its not always comprehending leader.[46] He had been forced by circumstances

---

[41] But note the striking parallels between the account of the Aldersgate heartwarming and an earlier experience in connection with William Law's *Practical Treatise Upon Christian Perfection* (1726) and *A Serious Call to a Devout and Holy Life* (1729): 'The light flowed in so mightily upon my soul that everything appeared in a new view. I cried to God for help . . . and I was persuaded that I *should be* accepted of him and that I was *even then* in a state of salvation.' (*JWJ*, May 24, 1738, §§5, 14). See also *A Plain Account of Christian Perfection*, §§4–5.

[42] He had already been scheduled for this engagement in St. Mary's; the university officials had had no way of knowing how different this new sermon would be from his last one there. See *JWJ*, May 28, June 11, which contains no notice of his sermon in St. Mary's.

[43] *JWJ*, Oct. 9: 'I read the truly surprising narrative of the conversions lately wrought in and about the town of Northampton, in New England. Surely "this is the Lord's doing, and it is marvellous in our eyes"!'

[44] See above, p. 14.

[45] This assurance, however, was not constant, as we can see from *JWJ*, Jan. 4, 1739: 'That I am not a Christian at this day I as assuredly know as that Jesus is the Christ.'

[46] See his description of his feelings of being 'swept along' (*pheromenos*) by events, letter of June 27, 1766 to his brother.

to rely on lay assistants as colleagues in this new 'extraordinary' ministry; doctrinal pluralism had followed from this as a matter of course. Wesley's reaction was to institute an annual gathering of the preachers, by his personal invitation, into a 'Conference' in which questions of doctrine and discipline were canvassed and worked through. Increasingly, however, the need for more and more doctrinal guidance became evident, and again Wesley responded, not with a creed or a confession, or even a doctrinal treatise, but with something analogous to a set of Methodist 'Homilies'—not in this case 'appointed to be read in the churches' (as Cranmer's had been) but rather to be studied and discussed by the Methodists and their critics. This decision that a cluster of *sermons* might serve as doctrinal standards for a popular religious movement is a significant revelation of Wesley's self-understanding of his role as spiritual director of 'the people called Methodists'. Sermons, as a genre, do not lend themselves to legalistic interpretation; these sermons in particular were the distillates of eight years of popular preaching and of a vigorous popular reaction. Wesley explains his motives in a crucial Preface which reads as if addressed as much to his non-Methodist critics as to his own disciples.

For his general title he resorted to an irony that would not have been lost on any well-read Anglican: *Sermons on Several Occasions*. This was, as they knew, a wholly conventional entitlement for sermons preached by ecclesiastical dignitaries in palaces and cathedrals.[47] Wesley's occasions had been far humbler; he was suggesting that they were not a whit less important. It is equally clear that his original design for this sermon series was open-ended. His first project was for a three-volume set of thirty-six sermons—1746, 1748, 1750. But as the revival burgeoned, so also there were new occasions for still more published sermons. Thus, in 1760, Wesley produced a fourth volume with the same title, but at first unnumbered; it is a curious medley of seven occasional sermons plus six paranetic tracts.[48]

---

[47] See, e.g., Anthony Tuckney, *Forty Sermons on Several Occasions* (1676); William Bates, *Sermons Preached on Several Occasions* (1693); John Sharp, *Sermons Preached on Several Occasions* (1700); John Scott, *Sermons Upon Several Occasions* (1704); William Tilly, *Sixteen Sermons . . . Preach'd Before the University of Oxford . . . Upon Several Occasions* (1712); John Tillotson, *Sermons on Several Occasions* (1671); George Smalridge, *Sixty Sermons Preached on Several Occasions* (1724); William Reeves, *Fourteen Sermons Preached on Several Occasions* (1729); John Rogers, *Nineteen Sermons on Several Occasions* (1735)—we have identified at least twenty such collections thus entitled.

[48] (1) 'Advice to the People Called Methodists, with Regard to Dress'; Wesley later (1786) published a sermon on this topic (see Sermon 88); (2) 'The Duties of Husbands and Wives', extracted from William Whateley, *A Bride-Bush; Or, a Direction for Married Persons* (1619); (3) and (4), 'Directions to Children' and 'Directions to Servants', were probably paraphrased by Wesley from William Gouge (see *Works . . . in two volumes: the first, Domes-*

This brought the number of *Sermons* to forty-three—still with no suggestion that they were legal documents; otherwise, the inclusion of those tracts would make no good sense. Later (the details are hazy), a forty-fourth sermon (Sermon 41, *Wandering Thoughts*) turned up in the second edition of Volume 3, published about 1763.[49] Meanwhile (1755), Wesley had provided his people with a specially designed exegetical tool for their biblical studies: his own revision of the AV New Testament with brief *Explanatory Notes*. These notes were partly original but also partially borrowed from other commentaries that he had found useful.[50] Thus, when problems of doctrinal variance among the Methodist preachers became acute enough, Wesley already had a practical solution. In the first trust deed of the Newcastle Orphan House (1746) he had specified in clearly nonforensic language that preaching in that chapel must be 'in the same manner, as near as may be, as God's Holy Word is now preached and expounded there' (i.e., by the Wesleys). By 1762 the situation called for something more precise, and in 1763 Wesley supplied it: a 'Model Deed' that set forth a sort of negative norm for Methodist orthodoxy, though still open-ended in principle. The trustees of the Methodist chapels were enjoined to welcome preachers appointed by Mr. Wesley, provided that they 'preach no other doctrine than is contained in Mr. Wesley's *Notes Upon the New Testament* and the four volumes of Sermons'.[51]

In the autumn of 1753 Wesley had been ill enough to feel prompted to

---

tical duties, 1627); (5) 'Thoughts on Christian Perfection', the Preface of which is dated, Bristol, Oct. 16, 1759, and later (1766) incorporated in *A Plain Account of Christian Perfection*; (6) 'Christian Instructions, Extracted from a Late French Author'.

[49] It was inserted, without explanation, between the sermon, *Christian Perfection* and the one on 'Satan's Devices'. One may guess that it had been written in 1761 (or early 1762), that it had been printed as a separate pamphlet by Felix Farley in 1762, and had then been quietly added to the new edition of *Sermons*. Its obvious function is to serve as a qualifying comment on the rather ambitious claims that had been registered in the sermon on *Christian Perfection*. Here again, we are reminded of the open-ended character of the *Sermons* project.

[50] E.g., Matthew Henry, *An Exposition of All the Books of the Old and New Testament* (1725); Matthew Poole, *Annotations Upon the Holy Bible* (1696); John Guyse, *A Practical Exposition of the Four Evangelists, in the Form of a Paraphrase, with Occasional Notes*, 3 vols. (1739–52); John Heylyn, *Theological Lectures, With an Interpretation of the Four Gospels*, 2 vols. (1749, 1751); Philip Doddridge, *Family Expositor; Or a Paraphrase and Version of the New Testament, with notes* (1739); and J. A. Bengel, *Gnomon Novi Testamenti* (1742).

[51] This comment first appeared in the Large Minutes of 1763, and was maintained verbatim in all succeeding versions. Taken literally, it could have been construed as giving the six paranetic tracts in vol. 4 an authoritative status of some sort; Wesley obviously never intended this—further proof that not even his Model Deed had to be construed constrictively.

compose his own epitaph.[52] In October of 1759 he spoke of 'the fourth volume of discourses' as 'probably the last which I shall publish'.[53] Actually, the growth rate of the Methodist societies and chapels quickened markedly after 1760,[54] and Wesley's health and vigour returned. Inevitably, then, he continued to write and publish new sermons, seeking always to refine and reinforce his basic doctrines. Nine of these new sermons appeared between 1758 (Sermon 15, *The Great Assize*) and 1770 (Sermon 53, *On the Death of George Whitefield*). Two of them are landmark sermons, crucial for any analysis of Wesley's maturing theology: *viz.*, Sermon 43, *The Scripture Way of Salvation* (1765)—a clear advance beyond Sermon 5, 'Justification by Faith'—and Sermon 20, *The Lord Our Righteousness* (1765), Wesley's clearest statement of the essential differences between his own soteriology and that of the English Calvinists.[55]

In 1770 he set out to finish a long-considered major project: the collection and ordering of those writings and publications of his which he now regarded as most fully representative: *The Works of the Rev. John Wesley, M. A., Late Fellow of Lincoln College, Oxford.*[56] His estimate of the *Sermons* by this time is suggested by the fact that he placed them at the head of his edition (vols. 1–4), with the nine new sermons inserted here and there (together with the tracts from the original vol. 4).[57] In his Preface he speaks of this new and personally authorized edition as reflecting his 'last and maturest thoughts, agreeable, I hope, to Scripture, reason, and Christian antiquity'. The inference is plain: at the heyday of his career (age 68) Wesley's own preferred order for the four volumes of *Sermons* was as we are presenting them here.

Despite unending controversy, and in some degree because of it, the

---

[52] 'To prevent vile panegyric'; see *JWJ*, Nov. 26 (but see also the longer period between early October 1753 and mid-April 1754).

[53] *JWJ*, Oct. 1.

[54] There were 31 chapels 'in connexion with Mr. Wesley' in 1760, 126 in 1771; see William Myles, *A Chronological History of the People Called Methodists*, 4th edition, (London, 1813), 427–45.

[55] Seven of the nine sermons produced from 1758 to 1770 reflect the theological transition from the 'middle Wesley' (1738–65) to the 'late Wesley' (1765–91): Sermons 15, *The Great Assize* (1758); 13, *On Sin in Believers* (1763); 43, *The Scripture Way of Salvation* (1765); 20, *The Lord Our Righteousness* (1765); 11, *The Witness of the Spirit*, II (1767); 14, *The Repentance of Believers* (1767); 51, *The Good Steward* (1768). The other two were occasional in the more literal sense: Sermons 52, *The Reformation of Manners* (1763), and 53, *On the Death of George Whitefield* (1770).

[56] *Works*, 32 vols. (Bristol, Pine, 1771–74).

[57] Except that in the new vol. 4 the tract on 'Christian Instructions' was replaced by 'An Extract from [the first five chs. of] Mr. Law's Treatise on *Christian Perfection*'.

Methodist Revival continued to flourish. In 1778 Wesley felt goaded enough to counterattack with a magazine frankly aimed at his Calvinist critics.[58] The first three volumes of this mélange had no sermons of Wesley's. In 1781, however, he began to include a numbered series of 'Original Sermons by the Rev. John Wesley, M. A.'; they appeared in installments (half a sermon per issue, or six in each annual volume). Six years later a rumour reached him that a clergyman 'in the West of England . . . designed to print, in two or three volumes, the sermons which had been published in the ten volumes of the *Arminian Magazine*'. To forestall this he undertook yet another edition of *Sermons*, explaining that if there were any call for such a thing he was 'the properest person to do it'.[59] Thus, in 1788 his new (and last) collection of sermons appeared, a hundred sermons in eight volumes. In Volumes 1–4, however, Wesley reverted to his earlier ordering, as before 1771, with eight of the nine additional sermons in the *Works* omitted, apparently discarded.[60] The decisive consideration here may have been the fact that to a certain degree since 1763, and especially after the legal establishment of 'The Conference' in 1784, 'the first four volumes of sermons' had acquired a legal role in what was virtually a new denomination.[61] In terms of any overview of Wesley's theology, the omission of these eight sermons would represent a serious loss.

In the Preface to *Sermons* 1 (1746), Wesley had explained: 'By the advice and at the request of some of my friends, I have prefixed to the other sermons contained in this volume three sermons of my own and one of my brother's, preached before the university of Oxford.'[62] These four sermons

---

[58] *The Arminian Magazine: Consisting of Extracts and Original Treatises on Universal Redemption.* vol. 1, For the Year 1778: 'Our design is to publish some of the most remarkable tracts on the universal love of God, and his willingness to *save all men* from *all sin*, which have been wrote in this and the last century. Some of these are now grown very scarce; some have not appeared in English before. To these will be added original pieces, wrote either directly upon this subject or on those which are equally opposed by the patrons of "particular redemption"' (§4).

[59] *Sermons* 5 (1788), Preface, §1.

[60] The sole exception was *The Lord Our Righteousness*, retained in vol. 3.

[61] Technically, the Methodists were still a religious society within the Church of England; actually, they were already on their way to eventual separation and their division into a congeries of separate denominations; see Frank Baker, *John Wesley and the Church of England*, 283–303; see also John S. Simon, *John Wesley, the Last Phase* (London, 1934), 19–22. See also 'The Deed of Declaration' of 1784, and Curnock 8:335–41. For a lively account of the protracted debate over the number of Wesley's 'standard sermons' and for its legal solution for the Methodists, see John S. Simon, 'The First Four Volumes of Wesley's Sermons', in *WHS* 9 (1913):36–45; see also Sugden, 'The Conference and the Fifty-three Sermons', 2:331–40.

[62] Preface, §7.

and their particular placement served two related purposes: first, they were manifestoes of the 'new' doctrine of 'faith alone'; second, they were signals of the pair's rejection of 'the groves of Academe' in favour of their new ministries to the English underclass.[63]

Wesley was not exaggerating when he claimed that these sermons (thirty-six, or forty-three, or forty-four) contained the gist of his understanding of 'the essentials of religion'.[64] The twelve sermons in Volume 1 (1746) are variations on the theme of his distinctive soteriology: salvation by unmerited grace, justification by faith as pardon and reconciliation, personal assurance of God's mercy confirmed by an 'inner witness of the Holy Spirit'. In the augmented edition of 1771 (the order followed here) one of the four added sermons is a revised formulation of the doctrine of *The Witness of the Spirit*; the second and third are rejections of all doctrines of guiltless 'perfection' (Sermons 13, *On Sin in Believers* and 14, *The Repentance of Believers*); the fourth is Wesley's sole *concio ad magistratum* (Sermon 15, *The Great Assize*). Volume 2 is concerned with the right 'order of salvation', from 'The Circumcision of the Heart' (Sermon 17) to the outworkings of faith in holy living (including Sermon 50, 'The Use of Money'). This is why, in the edition of 1771, Wesley could insert *The Lord Our Righteousness* (Sermon 20) between a sermon on the restoration of the power not to commit wilful sin (Sermon 19, 'The Great Privilege of those that are Born of God') and the true centrepiece of the whole collection (*viz.*, his thirteen-sermon series 'Upon Our Lord's Sermon on the Mount'), followed by a three-sermon series on the positive correlations of Law and Gospel.[65] The central thesis throughout this series is that the Law had served a proto-Christological function and, therefore, that the 'law' of 'love' continues to

---

[63] See *JWJ*, Aug. 24, 1744 ('St. Bartholomew's Day'): 'I preached, I suppose, the last time at St. Mary's. Be it so. I am now clear of the blood of these men. I have fully delivered my own soul' (see Ezek. 3:9). This last phrase is used by Wesley invariably as an expression of frustration and rejection. See *JWJ*, June 9, 1779, and Apr. 2, 1787; see his letter to the Mayor of Newcastle upon Tyne, July 12, 1743, to William Law, Jan. 6, 1756, and to Mary Bishop, May 27, 1771; and see Sermon 88, 'On Dress', §22. It is true that Wesley did not resign his Lincoln fellowship or its stipend until forced to do so by his marriage in 1751. But after 1744 all his effective ties with Oxford were severed, and more on his own initiative than that of the university.

[64] Preface, §1. When Wesley first spoke of his sermons thus, he had only three vols.—and thirty-six sermons—in prospect (see the title-page of *Sermons* 1 (1746)). The addition of a fourth volume (1760) resulted in forty-three sermons. By 1763, with the addition of 'Wandering Thoughts' to the second edition of volume three, the phrase denoted forty-four. The project remained open-ended in his own mind.

[65] Sermons 34–36, 'The Original, Nature, Properties, and Use of the Law': 'The Law Established through Faith, I'; and 'The Law Established through Faith, II'.

define the essence and end of Christian existence. Volume 3 is a sort of ellipse with its twin foci Wesley's understanding of the graciousness of grace (Sermon 39, 'Catholic Spirit') and the fullness of grace (Sermon 40, *Christian Perfection*). The resultant view of Christian living is brought into a balanced conspectus in the added sermon on *The Scripture Way of Salvation* (Sermon 43); the other sermons deal with one or another facet of this larger view. In the edition of 1771 there are three new and literally occasional sermons: *The Good Steward*, *The Reformation of Manners*, and Wesley's memorial sermon for George Whitefield (Sermons 51–53).

Even a casual analysis of these 'first four volumes of sermons' reveals that questions of chronology and provenance are incidental. Their order is shaped by the inner logic of Wesley's special view of the mystery of salvation. It is in this sense that they may rightly be regarded as a normative statement of the foundations of Wesleyan soteriology, even if not as his complete account of Christian existence.[66]

Sermons on Several Occasions, *Volumes 5–8 (1788)*

As he approached his own 'three-score years and ten', Wesley took heart from the fact that the Revival had outlasted a generation.[67] As we have seen in the case of the Methodist chapels,[68] the Methodist movement grew more rapidly in its second generation than in its first, and its general impact on English society became more and more noticeable.[69] What has

---

[66] Henry Moore, one of Wesley's closest friends, summarized them thus: '[Wesley's] first four volumes contain the substance of what he usually declared in the pulpit. He designed by them to give a view of what St. Paul calls . . . "the analogy of faith", *viz.*, the strong connection and harmony between those grand fundamental doctrines, original sin, justification by faith in the divine atonement of the Son of God, the new birth, inward and outward holiness.' (Moore 2:405.) See also J. A. Beet's compact summary of the theological problem of the so-called Wesleyan 'standards' in 'The First Four Volumes of Wesley's Sermons', *WHS* 9 (1913):86–89.

[67] See Sermon 63, 'The General Spread of the Gospel', §16 (and n.), where Wesley quotes Luther as having said a revival 'never lasts above a generation, that is, thirty years (whereas the present revival has already continued above fifty)'; see also Sermons 94, 'On Family Religion', §3; and 122, 'Causes of the Inefficacy of Christianity', §17.

[68] See above, p. 51, n. 54.

[69] E.g., the *Minutes* of 1767 records a total of 25,911 members in all the Societies in England, Ireland, Scotland, and Wales (not really a mass movement even when it is remembered that this is a carefully winnowed membership list). In 1791 this same statistic had nearly trebled for the British Isles (to 72,476), together with 6,525 members in the missionary societies in 'The British Dominions' of America. To these were added the 57,621 reported members in 'The United States', giving a grand total of 136,622. For a comment on the social visibility and impact of the Methodists in this last third of Wesley's

been less carefully noted is that Wesley, in the last two decades of his life, was even more productive than before both of written sermons and of edited materials for his people. This was the period of his collected *Works* (1771-74), of the *Arminian Magazine* (1778-91), and of the pamphlet war with Calvinists.[70] But more, it was a time of still further theological maturation, especially in the development of his views of Christian praxis. It is as if, after laying the firm foundations of his soteriology, Wesley had set himself to work out its practical consequences—without weakening any of those foundations. And yet it is just this rich vein of Wesley's *thought* that has suffered the most neglect in Wesley studies generally, even though such ancillary questions as his churchmanship (the Deed of Declaration and his ordinations) have been pored over endlessly. The sermons from these last two decades are, therefore, of great importance for any rounded view of his vision of the Christian life. This is why his second collection of *Sermons* (Volumes 5-8) is so much more than an addendum to Volumes 1-4. They reveal new, and some fresh, facets of Wesley's mind and heart, and lend further complications to any explanation of his role as folk-theologian.

As we have seen, the decision to collect and publish these last four volumes came late (1787). It was taken under pressure, and the project itself was carried out in evident haste. But he had conserved a rich store of sermon manuscripts that he had been writing as 'original sermons' since 1775 and publishing in the *Arminian Magazine* since 1781. Incidentally, the ordering of the sermons as published in the *Arminian Magazine* differs from the order of their composition. The sequence of *Sermons* 5-8 differs still further. There is an ambiguous comment on this in his Preface. There he says, quite straightforwardly (§3): 'To make these plain discourses more useful, I purpose now to range [this series of fifty-six sermons] in proper order; placing those first which are intended to throw light on some important Christian doctrines, and afterwards those which more directly relate

---

life see Semmel, *Methodist Revolution*, chs. 1, 4. See also Stuart Andrews, *Methodism and Society* (London, 1970), chs. 1 and 2.

[70] In this he was vigorously assisted by John William Fletcher, Walter Sellon, Thomas Olivers, and others. Fletcher (1729-85) was the Swiss-born and educated vicar of Madeley in Shropshire, and erstwhile president of the Countess of Huntingdon's college at Trevecca, Wales. He became embroiled in the controversy after 1770 and published a series of five *Checks to Antinomianism* in 1774 and 1775, and *The Doctrines of Grace and Justice Equally Essential to the Pure Gospel* in 1777. Walter Sellon, another Anglican priest, published a number of pamphlets for John Goodwin and against Augustus Toplady and Elisha Cole in the period of 1774 and thereafter; they are most easily consulted in his *Works*, 2 vols. (London, 1814-15). Thomas Olivers (1725-99) entered the lists against Toplady and the brothers Hill; see his *Full Defence of the Rev. John Wesley. . . .* (1776), *A Defence of Methodism. . . .* (1785), and *A Full Refutation . . . of Unconditional Perseverance* (1790).

to some branch of Christian practice. And I shall endeavour to place them all in such an order that one may illustrate and confirm the other.' Actually, however, he begins Volume 5 with two of the most speculative sermons he ever wrote (Sermons 54, 'On Eternity', dated June 28, 1786, and 55, *On the Trinity*, dated May 7, 1775). The sequence thereafter seems somewhat more random than cumulative. He claims the right to alter his own texts at will, 'either to retrench what is redundant, to supply what is wanting, or to make any farther alterations which shall appear needful' (§2). Actually, the variations between the texts as they had appeared in the *Arminian Magazine* and again in *Sermons* 5-8 are negligible on points of substance. Also in this second Preface (to 5), he reviews his praise of 'plain style' and his disparagement of 'French oratory'. And yet it will quickly be noticed that these late sermons are more copiously 'ornamented' (with classical tags, poetry, obscure quotations, and learned references) than any of the earlier sermons. Moreover, there is no explanation whatever of his omission of the extra sermons in *Works* (1771), 1-4, or of his salvaging of *The Lord Our Righteousness* from that group.

What is most striking about these late sermons is their range, as well as their reflection of Wesley's intense concern for all the practical aspects of 'contemporary Christian living'. Obviously, they are the work of an aging man, preoccupied with the pressures of the Revival. Their quality is uneven and only a few (Sermons 62, 'The End of Christ's Coming'; 73, 'Of Hell'; 85, 'On Working Out Our Own Salvation'; 115, 'Dives and Lazarus'; and 127, 'On the Wedding Garment') represent significant reformulations of older ideas. And yet there is nothing senescent in their spirit and nothing outdated in their sensitivity to current issues. They are the results of the aging Wesley's efforts to integrate the evangelical soteriology already established in *Sermons* 1-4 with the sort of theology of culture he could see that his 'plain people' needed. There are sermons here to fortify and edify believers in the face of new challenges to historic Christian doctrine from Enlightenment scepticism and secularism. There is ammunition here for the Methodists in their protracted debates with the Calvinists, on one flank, and Anglican traditionalists, on the other. Their primary audience is the growing company of mature Christians long since converted, but newly confounded with new perplexities, in urgent need of wise pastoral counsel about their actual tasks in a changing world. Most specifically, as Wesley saw with increasing alarm, the earlier Methodist zeal for stewardship was lagging among those whose thrift, industry, and sobriety had rewarded them with unaccustomed affluence. These late sermons are mirrors to an age in which the ideas of Adam Smith's *Wealth of Nations* (published in 1776) were gaining the status of economic dogma; in their stress on surplus accumulation these 'new' ideas directly contradicted Wesley's 'third rule' for 'the use of money'—*viz.*, 'Give all you can.' It is no accident, therefore, that he would denounce surplus accumulation more frequently—and more stridently.

At the heart of all these practical counsels about the Christian family, 'attending the church services', 'the imperfections of human knowledge', etc., lay a rich and complex doctrine of *free grace* and its implications for a Christian's everyday problems of loving God above all else and of loving one's neighbour (defined as 'every child of man'). They suggest that Wesley may have had in mind something of an analogy between these late sermons and one or more of the classical manuals of Christian praxis that he knew had served earlier generations of English Christians so well—Richard Baxter's *Poor Man's Family Book* (1674), Jeremy Taylor's *Ductor Dubitantium* (1660), or *The Whole Duty of Man* (1657), probably by Richard Allestree. Indeed, Wesley had published an extensive 'extract' of *The Whole Duty of Man* in his *Christian Library*, 21:3-194, with a significant foreword 'To the Reader':

> Whoever reads the following treatise should consider the time wherein it was wrote [*viz.*, the Cromwellian Commonwealth]. Never was there more talk of faith in Christ, of justification by faith, and of the fruits of the Spirit. And scarce ever was there less practice of plain, moral duties, of justice, mercy, and truth. At such a time it was peculiarly needful to inculcate what was so generally neglected. . . .
>
> I do not apprehend that any one page herein contradicts that fundamental principle, 'By grace ye are saved through faith', being justified freely 'through the redemption which is in Jesus'. Nor am I afraid that any who have read the preceding volumes should be induced by any part of this to build again the things which they had thrown down, to seek salvation by their own righteousness. But I trust, many who have already experienced the free grace of God in Christ Jesus may hereby be more fully instructed to walk in him, and more thoroughly furnished for every good word and work.

Something like this may be said of the whole of *Sermons* 5-8; it enlarges the notion of pastoral theology in a fresh and edifying way.

The Other Sermons

Meanwhile, between 1739 and 1788 Wesley published five sermons which he never included in any of his collections. They are not negligible items in the corpus, but, for various reasons, they did not fit the 'logic' of any of Wesley's orderings. The first of these was his intemperate attack on George Whitefield's doctrine of 'the decrees' in 1739 (Sermon 110, *Free*

Grace). This had caused a breach between the two that never thereafter was fully healed despite a wary sort of reconciliation and a tenuous relationship that Wesley managed with Whitefield's patroness, the Countess of Huntingdon, until 1770. Moreover, Wesley was invited, by Whitefield's prior designation, to preach his 'official' memorial sermon in the two London 'Tabernacles' on November 18, 1770. Wesley must have realized, therefore, that republishing *Free Grace* in *Sermons on Several Occasions* would serve no good purpose. It was Joseph Benson who decided that it should be included in his edition of Wesley's *Works* (1809–13), vol. 8, (but without the long poem that Charles had written to match the sermon's prose). Thomas Jackson simply followed Benson's lead both in his separate edition of the *Sermons* in 1825 (vol. 1), and in the collected *Works* of 1829–31 (vol. 7).

No other such maverick sermon appeared till 1775, when Wesley published a charity sermon preached by invitation in St. Matthew's, Bethnal Green, on November 12, 'for the benefit of the widows and orphans of the soldiers who lately fell near Boston, in New England'. The reference here was to the opening skirmishes of the American Revolution (April 19 and June 17, 1775). In this sermon, on 2 Sam. 24:17, besides his incidental criticisms of the rebellious Americans, Wesley expounds a long-standing Christian platitude: a nation's miseries are usually the fruits of that nation's sins.[71] There was, however, no obvious place for it in *Sermons* 5–8, and Benson may have overlooked it. Thomas Jackson decided that it should not be lost, and included it in both of his editions (Sermon 58 in that of 1825; Sermon 130 in *Works* of 1829–31, vol. 7) and supplied the title still retained here, *National Sins and Miseries.*

Much earlier—indeed, shortly after *Free Grace*—Wesley had written two sermons that fall outside our category of published sermons but may be mentioned here. They were bold denunciations of hypocrisy in Oxford (or maybe the same sermon in a Latin and an English version). They may have been connected with the exercises for the B.D. degree he was expected to take as a Fellow of Lincoln. Very prudently, he published neither (and was never awarded the B.D. degree, either), but nevertheless he preserved them in his papers. What little we know about their history is sketched out above,[72] but what needs to be noted here is that they belong to that strange love-hate relationship that Wesley had with Oxford, and that they are also the most convincing demonstration we have of his facility and actual eloquence in Neo-Ciceronian Latin. Benson may not even have

---

[71] For a review of how the Puritans had rung the changes on this same theme, see John Wilson, *Pulpit in Parliament.*

[72] See p. 40ff.

known of them; the English version appeared in Jackson's 'Fifth Series' with its triumphalist title, 'True Christianity Defended'.[73] The Latin version is published for the first time in the Bicentennial Edition of the *Sermons.*

In 1777 Wesley wrote and published a truly 'occasional' sermon which he omitted from *Sermons* 5-8. Its occasion was the laying of the foundation for his new Chapel in the City Road, April 21.[74] This was an interesting move away from the old Foundery on 'Windmill Hill' (which had served as his London centre since 1739) to a much more impressive headquarters closer to Whitefield's fine brick Tabernacle[75] and directly across City Road from the Nonconformist cemetery of Bunhill Fields.[76] It was natural enough that, given such a new beginning with its inescapable sectarian overtones, Wesley would be prompted to a somewhat complacent review of his particular movement and to a mildly triumphalist reflection upon its prospects. The sermon was published shortly thereafter, and as promptly denounced by the Rev. Rowland Hill, Minister of Surrey Chapel, Blackfriars Road.[77]

In the year following Wesley wrote and published a sermon on Ezek. 1:16 which he himself entitled, *Some Account of the Late Work of God in North America.* Tyerman judged it 'almost a misnomer to designate this a sermon';[78] it is, however, an exposition of one of Wesley's favourite themes: 'the adorable providence of God' in the midst of tragic circumstance. In it he deplores the American rebellion and then turns seer to prophesy a British victory which would 'make way for the happy return of [the Americans to their erstwhile] humility, temperance, industry, and chastity'. The sermon was popular enough to run through four printings in 1778, but history quickly outran the prophecy; it was not published again until the Jackson edition of 1825 and, again, slightly revised, in 1829.

---

[73] See his edition of the *Works* (1829-31), 7:451, where Jackson sees only a martyr's heroic courage: 'To deliver such a sermon before that learned body [more probably in The Divinity School than in St. Mary's if, indeed, it were ever "delivered"] required no small degree of pious resolution; it is a striking display of that spirit of sacrifice by which Mr. Wesley was actuated.'

[74] See *JWJ*, Apr. 21, 1777, and Curnock's note. For a detailed account of this event and its history, see George J. Stevenson, *City Road Chapel* (London, 1873).

[75] See Seymour 1:198-202, for the history of the modest beginning of the 'Tabernacle' in 1741 (a large 'shed') to its more spacious rebuilding in 1752-53.

[76] The Meeting-House and burying ground of the London Society of Friends (grave of George Fox) is only some fifty yards farther west of Bunhill Fields.

[77] In his *Imposture Detected* (1777); see above, p. 30, n. 35. See *Works* 9:402-15 for Wesley's *Answer.*

[78] *Wesley* 3:280.

The one other sermon that Wesley wrote and published in this period, but then omitted from his collection, was the memorial eulogy for his old friend and ally, John William Fletcher. Fletcher, 'Wesley's designated successor,'[79] had died in Madeley on August 14, 1785, while Wesley was on his itinerant rounds in Wiltshire and the West of England. He had returned to London on November 4 and on the sixth had delivered the eulogy in his bright new chapel. As may be seen, its emphasis was biographical; Wesley had based it on materials furnished him by Fletcher's wife, the former Mary Bosanquet.[80] Wesley had it published within the year, and it was widely reprinted thereafter.[81] However, it was not included in *Sermons* 5–8; it appeared again in Benson, and in Jackson's 'Fourth Series'.

Even after the publication of *Sermons* 5–8, Wesley continued to write and publish sermons. These appeared in the *Arminian Magazine* from May–June, 1789, through July–August, 1792, in a somewhat random order as far as any substantive logic may be discerned, but still in the numbered series as before. In 1800 George Story collected seventeen of these 'new' sermons in a posthumous ninth volume of *Sermons* in the same order as in the *Arminian Magazine*, *except* for Wesley's sermon on Heb. 5:4, in which he had defended his longtime practice of forbidding his lay preachers to administer the sacraments.[82] By 1800 the Methodists were in no mood to be edified by an argument of this sort; Story, therefore, simply dropped it out, leaving Thomas Jackson to 'restore' it in his edition of the *Works* (1829–31, vol. 7), with, however, an explicit disavowal of its main thesis.

These very late sermons display the same intent and something of the quality of their predecessors. The most remarkable of them is Sermon 127, 'On the Wedding Garment', in which Wesley openly rejects the Puritan interpretation of 'the wedding garment' as 'the spotless robe of Christ's righteousness', imputed to us vicariously as our own, but rather as that 'holiness' itself, 'without which no man shall see the Lord.' Here, finally, the venerable evangelist comes back round to the same motif he had expounded so long ago in 'The Circumcision of the Heart'.[83] It is the end-

---

[79] See Luke Tyerman's biography of Fletcher with this title (London, 1882).

[80] See her *Letter to the Rev. Mr. Wesley on the Death of the Rev. Mr. Fletcher, Vicar of Madeley*, dated Aug. 18, 1785, and printed by J. Edmunds of Madeley; see also her other letter to her husband's brother which was published in 1786: *A Letter to Mons. H. L. de la Flechere . . . on the death of his brother, the Reverend John William de la Flechere, twenty-five years vicar of Madeley, Shropshire.*

[81] *Works* (1829–31), Sermon 133.

[82] See Sermon 121, 'Prophets and Priests' (and introductory comment). It was promptly dubbed 'the Korah sermon' and openly criticized by Henry Moore and others; see Moore 2:338–40.

[83] See Sermon 17.

point of a convoluted 'progress'—from faith in faith to faith in grace.

Three sermons that could not be included in the Wesley corpus on the same terms as the others still deserve our passing notice here. The first is one on 'The Cause and Cure of Earthquakes', a topic of general interest to all eighteenth-century defenders of God's good providence in nature.[84] Jackson published it as John's: 'no doubt can be entertained about its being the production of Mr. Wesley's pen.'[85] The 'Mr. Wesley' in question, however, turns out to have been Charles, who could, on such a question, have spoken for both brothers.[86]

A second sermon that has traditionally been attributed to Wesley with insufficient evidence is a stenographic transcription of what is said to have been Wesley's sermon on the occasion of the opening 'of the new house at Wakefield', April 28, 1774.[87] The transcript was made in shorthand 'at the time of delivery' and then promptly published 'at the request of many hearers'.[88] If we could be certain of this text (if, e.g., we had Wesley's corroboration of it or his inclusion of it in any collection), we would have to reckon with its indication that at least some of Wesley's oral sermons were remarkably similar to his written texts in both rhetoric and substance—except that this one is duller than most. As the data stand now, however, this text had better be classified as dubious, which is not to say 'spurious'.

Another instance of an interesting text that remains uncertain is a manuscript sermon on Heb. 4:9 that was published by Albert F. Hall in *The London Quarterly and Holborn Review*, 165 (April 1940):139–46. Earlier efforts to locate the manuscript for collation proved unavailing; it was not included in the papers and books bequeathed by Mr. Hall to Lincoln College in 1972. It has, however, finally surfaced, and is now in the collection of Perkins School of Theology. The text is apparently in John Wesley's hand, but in substance it turns out to be a sort of homiletical outline of Richard Baxter's *Saints' Everlasting Rest*. In form it is original, and might well have been published in full in the Bicentennial Edition of the *Sermons*. In substance, however, it ranks with other 'extracts' by Wesley from his fa-

---

[84] It was an example of an extensive sermonic literature occasioned by the London earthquakes of Feb. 8 and Mar. 8, 1750; see, e.g., William Whiston, *Memoirs, . . . to which are added his lectures on the late remarkable meteors and earthquakes. . .*, 2nd edition, 1753), Part 3, 216–20. See *JWJ* for the above dates; see also Moore 2:158–59, whose vivid description of London's panic reaction to these quakes includes an account of Whitefield's preaching at midnight to crowds who had flocked together in Hyde Park.

[85] See Editor's Preface to *Wesley's Sermons* (1825).

[86] See *CWJ*, Mar. 9, 1750; see also his *Hymns Occasioned by the Earthquake* (1750).

[87] See *JWJ*: 'So I preached in the main street [of Wakefield]. . .'.

[88] See *Works* 4:519–24.

vorite authors.[89] Its chief significance is as a further testimony to Baxter's influence on Wesley's thought.

A Conspectus

From any such survey of the development of Wesley's sermon corpus, at least five general conclusions emerge that lend support to the 'logic' of the order adopted in this present edition. The first is that Wesley himself understood *Sermons* 1–8 as definitive of his role as preacher, teacher, evangelist, and pastor. In two successive personal wills (in 1768 and again in 1789), he bequeathed a set of these sermons (first, in their four-volume format, the second, 'the eight volumes') 'to each travelling preacher who should remain in the connexion six months after [his] decease'.[90] Moreover, the Model Deed of 1763 continued in force in all the Methodist Chapels 'in connexion with Mr. Wesley'. A second reasonably clear conclusion is that Wesley's understanding of the *Sermons'* primary function was not as a legal instrument with a fixed, exclusive number of sermons intended for literal construction by title or canon lawyers. The title had an open-ended connotation; Wesley meant to allow for enlargement and development in his own unfolding thought and that of others. George Story was not presumptuous in his entitlement of the posthumous Volume 9 as *Sermons on Several Occasions*. By the same token, the miscellaneous sermons, both early and late, have an interest in their own right in any critical or comprehensive review of Wesley's thought. They expose his understanding of the 'order of salvation' (always his central concern) in other facets and dimensions that have yet to be probed and fully integrated into a fully-orbed study of his life and work. A fourth generalization may only reflect a personal impression that has grown firmer through the years: *viz.*, that the *later* Wesley is the neglected Wesley, and that a redress of this imbalance is sorely needed if the agenda of Wesley studies is ever to regain its due proportions. And, finally, the manuscript sermons here newly edited and published may add more than mere quantity to our resources for a critical reconstruction of the Wesleyan theology. Most of them are mediocre and one of them, 'Hypocrisy in Oxford', like the published *Free Grace*, reflects an uncatholic spirit. But the best of them ('The Image of God', 'The Wisdom of Winning Souls', 'The One Thing Needful', etc.) open up new facets of Wesley's early thought and later more than a few uncritical stereotypes.

---

[89] See *Works* 4:531–33.
[90] See Tyerman, *John Wesley* 3:15, 616–17; also Hampson, *Memoirs* 3:231–35.

It is admittedly awkward that each new edition of Wesley's sermons requires a new and different enumeration from any of its predecessors. This can scarcely be avoided. Not since *Wandering Thoughts* turned up unannounced in 1763, in the second edition of *Sermons* 3, has the problem of order and enumeration ever been as simple as an editor or reader might have preferred.

4. THEOLOGICAL METHOD
AND THE PROBLEMS OF DEVELOPMENT

It was Wesley's way to speak as directly as he could to his actual audiences; this is plain in his letters, polemical rejoinders, and essays, but most of all in his sermons.[1] This would follow from his conviction that preaching is the chief business of the evangelist, and it explains his choice of the sermon as the chief genre for his theological expositions. He understood the difference between the dialectical character of sermons and the didactic character of systematic treatises. Quite consciously, and from the beginning, he preferred the former. He knew as much as most of his contemporaries about the history of the creeds and confessions, but he seems never to have felt any compulsion to compose yet another creed or confession. It is noteworthy that in his sermons and letters he would, here and there, strike off apt summaries of the essence of Christian truth. But these are clearly distillates for edification rather than doctrinal formularies demanding a yes or no response. This general view of his role as preacher fitted well with his eclectic impulses as a theologian: he was a born borrower who nevertheless put his own mark on every borrowing. There is, therefore, a crucial methodological question as to whether in the sprawling array of his writings and editings there are consistent interests that amount to a coherent self-understanding. One of the aims of the Bicentennial Edition of his *Works* is to make it possible to sift such a question in a larger context.

It is important to begin with the recognition that Wesley's baseline tradition was Erasmian, as this particular perspective had been shaped through the course of the English Reformation (Bucer, Cranmer, Hooker) and the ensuing struggles between the Puritans and the Anglicans (Mede, Pearson, Beveridge). When hard-pressed by the Lutheran and Calvinist challenges (from the Moravians and from Edwards), Wesley fell back instinctively on Erasmians like Cranmer and Harpsfield.[2] This tradition involved a sincere

---

[1] Not even his *Explanatory Notes on the New Testament* are an exception to this rule (especially when compared to other commentaries) nor his one long treatise (*The Doctrine of Original Sin*), which is less a conventional essay than a protracted debate with a single disputant. All his other extracts reflect this same impulse toward personal address: he is always the preacher-teacher trying to edify a targeted clientele.

[2] But note his quite self-conscious balancing act of matching his extract from the Anglican *Homilies* with a similar extract from Barnes's *Two Treatises on Justification*; see above,

commitment to the ideals of Christian humanism (non-dogmatic in mood and style), open to an alliance between reverent faith and reverent learning, concerned above all else with a gracious Christian lifestyle. By Wesley's time, however, it had evolved into a gospel of moral rectitude, but still with its three professed guidelines: Scripture, reason, and Christian antiquity.[3] To this Wesley had added a strong element of mystical piety.[4] It was this that sustained his lifelong interest in the patristic ideal of divine-human 'participation'—expressed in every Eucharist in the Prayer of Humble Access: '. . . that we may evermore dwell in him, and he in us'.[5] Wesley brought to this complex heritage two new elements: the first, a distinctive stress on the primacy of Scripture (not merely as 'standing revelation'[6] but as a 'speaking book'); and, second, an insistence upon the personal assurance of God's justifying, pardoning grace (which is what he always meant by such terms as 'experience', 'experimental', 'heart religion'). The constant goal of Christian living, in his view, is sanctification ('Christian perfection' or 'perfect love'); its organizing principle is always the *order of salvation*; the divine agency in it all is the Holy Spirit. Thus it was that Wesley understood prevenience as the distinctive work of the Holy Spirit and as the primal force in all authentic spirituality. This perspective was expounded in unsystematic forms, and yet it was inwardly coherent and relatively consistent in its development. And it is this basic viewpoint that is to be looked for in all the sermons: early, middle, and late.

Wesley's point of departure was always Holy Scripture, understood according to the 'analogy of faith' (i.e., its general sense),[7] and as 'the standing revelation' in the Christian church throughout her long history. He had

---

p. 46, n. 36, for a discussion of Barnes.

[3] See Irène Simon, *Three Restoration Divines*, chs. 1-2; see also P. E. More and F. L. Cross, eds., *Anglicanism* (Milwaukee, 1935), ch. 5(2), pp. 132-41. See also Francis Paget, *An Introduction to the Fifth Book of Hooker's Ecclesiastical Polity*, 2nd edition (London, 1907), p. 284.

[4] See his review of his theological history to the end of 1737 in his memorandum of Jan. 25, 1738 (see Moore, 1:342-44). Note in this self-criticism of his overstress on tradition, his negative judgments on the Lutherans and Calvinists, and his discovery of the dangers of the mysticism which had nonetheless influenced him deeply and would continue to do so.

[5] See The Book of Common Prayer, Communion. Wesley's first discovery on the day of his Aldersgate experience was the promise in 2 Pet. 1:4, 'that ye should be partakers of the divine nature' (JWJ, May 24, 1738, §13). See also the review of the 'participation' theme in the patristic churches in David Bálàs, *Metousia Theou: Man's Participation in God's Perfection According to St. Gregory of Nyssa* (Rome, 1966).

[6] See Offspring Blackall, 'The Sufficiency of a Standing Revelation', Discourses 88-95, *Works* 2:941-1052—his Boyle Lectures for 1700.

[7] For Wesley's references to the 'analogy of faith', see Sermon 5, 'Justification by Faith', §2 and n.

grown up with Scripture as a second language; even in his early sermons one sees the beginnings of his lifelong habit of interweaving Scripture with his own speech in a graceful texture. Later, he will recall that it was not until 1729 that he began to be *homo unius libri*,[8] but this could only mean a rearrangement of priorities, not a novelty. There was never a thought that he should restrict his reading to the biblical text alone. It was, instead, a matter of hermeneutical principle that Scripture would be his court of first and last resort in faith and morals. This was the entire Scripture, too, and not just a biblical anthology; his view of the canon (not excluding the Apocrypha) was of a whole and integral revelation, inspired by the same Holy Spirit who continues to guide all serious readers into its unfathomable truth, parts and whole together. And it was from this basic doctrine of biblical inspiration that his main principles of interpretation were derived—all five of them. The first was that believers should accustom themselves to the biblical language and thus to the 'general sense' of Scripture as a whole. This general sense is omnipresent throughout the canon even if not equally so in every text; there is a 'message' in every part of Holy Writ, and it is always the same, in essence. This leads to a second rule, adapted from the ancient Fathers and from the Reformers as well: that the Scriptures are to be read as a whole, with the expectation that the clearer texts may be relied upon to illuminate the obscurer ones. There is no authority above Scripture from which a more definitive interpretation of revelation may be sought. Wesley was not indifferent to historical and literary questions in exegesis; he was living in the early days of the new biblical criticism, and he had a lively interest in the commentators (old and new).[9] But his constant focus was the text itself; his constant concern was with its direct address to the reader. Moreover, despite the fact that he had his favourite texts and passages in both Old and New Testaments, he had no 'canon within the canon'. This holistic sense of biblical inspiration suggested his third hermeneutical principle: that one's exegesis is to be guided, always in the first instance, by the literal sense, unless that appears to lead to consequencs that are either irrational or unworthy of God's moral character as 'pure, unbounded love'.[10] Then, and only with caution, the exegete may seek for an edifying

---

[8] In the Preface, §5, to *Sermons* 1 (1746), it is implied that his commitment to *sola Scriptura* came with the conversion of 1738. However, in a letter to William Dodd, Feb. 5, 1756, he speaks of his resolve 'to make the Scriptures my study about seven-and-twenty years ago' (i.e., 1729). This same dating is repeated in *A Plain Account of Christian Perfection* (1765), §§5, 10.

[9] For Wesley's indebtedness to Matthew Henry, Matthew Poole, John Heylyn, Philip Doddridge, *et al*, see above, p. 50, n. 50.

[10] See Sermon 21, 'Sermon on the Mount, I', §6 and n.

allegory or anagogy, but only within the terms of the analogy of faith. A fourth hermeneutical rule follows from his doctrine of grace and free will: that all moral commands in Scripture are also 'covered promises', since God never commands the impossible and his grace is always efficacious in every faithful will.[11] His last rule is actually a variation on the Anglican sense of the old Vincentian canon that the historical experience of the church, though fallible, is the better judge overall of Scripture's meanings than later interpreters are likely to be, especially on their own.[12] Thus, radical novelty is to be eschewed on principle.[13]

One of the bonuses of an Oxford education for most of its alumni was a living sense of the continuity of the past into the future. Wesley had had the additional advantage of an acquaintance with John Clayton, the ardent patrologist of the Holy Club.[14] This discovery of 'the Fathers of the Church' reinforced Wesley's natural tendency to set most of his problems in their historical perspectives; one cannot point to another popular theologian with as lively a sense of the normative role of Christian antiquity for contemporary theology. The sermons do not display their larger historical background, but it is almost always there; for the purposes of any critical analysis this background will almost always reward a careful probing.

This general approach to biblical hermeneutics presupposed (or required) a matching theory of religious knowledge if the interpreter was to avoid the open trap of literalism, on the one side, or traditionalism on the other. Here Wesley found himself in an interesting dilemma. He was an avowed empiricist[15] in an age of empiricism;[16] yet he was also an unembarrassed intuitionist who openly claimed his heritage of Christian Platonism. This had come to him more generally from the Fathers, William of St. Thierry, the Victorines, St. Bonaventura, and the Cambridge Platonists. More directly, however, he had been instructed by his father's friend, John Norris, and also by Richard Lucas. Norris was the chief English disciple of

---

[11] See Sermon 25, 'Sermon on the Mount, V', §II.2 and n.

[12] See Sermon 13, *On Sin in Believers*, §III.9 and n.; see also the memorandum for Jan. 25, 1738 (see p. 47, n. 38, above). The reference there is to *The Commonitory of Vincent of Lerins* (A.D. 435), ch. ii, §6.

[13] See Sermon 25, 'Sermon on the Mount, V', §1 and n.; and see also Sermon 17, 'The Circumcision of the Heart', §1.

[14] See V. H. H. Green, *The Young Mr. Wesley*, pp. 173–74.

[15] He repeats, almost casually, the Thomist formula that 'there is nothing in the mind not previously in the senses'; see Sermon 117, 'On the Discoveries of Faith', §1 and n.

[16] See Isaiah Berlin, ed., *The Age of Enlightenment: The 18th Century Philosophers* (New York, 1956); see also Frederick Copleston, *A History of Philosophy* (London, 1959), vol. 5, chs. 4–17; and Etienne Gilson and Thomas Langan, *Modern Philosophy: Descartes to Kant* (New York, 1963), chs. 12–14.

the French Cartesian, Nicholas Malebranche, and Wesley was more heavily influenced by Malebranche's 'occasionalism' than was any other eighteenth-century British theologian.[17]

He was reasonably well-versed in the history of 'natural philosophy'; he was very much aware of the knowledge explosion of his times; he shared the rationalist temper of his age; he was a trained logician. But he never supposed that theology was an empirical science, and he was careful to mark off the proper limits of reason.[18] He could, therefore, discuss the empirical 'orders of creation' in terms of a strictly empirical knowledge of tangible reality, and still insist that our knowledge of God and 'the things of God' must be intuitive, since reality at this level does not fall within the scope of empirical knowledge.

For even Locke himself had recognized a special domain for 'truths above reason'.[19] And thus, like many another dualist before him, Wesley drew what he thought was a clear line between our knowledge of things and our knowledge of spiritual reality; he found a persuasive analogy between our empirical sensorium and what he could think and speak of as our 'spiritual senses'. He understood how Descartes had conceived of our awareness of immaterial reality as truly primitive (*simplici mentis intuitu*); he knew Malebranche's variations on this theme. With a supporting tradition, therefore, he regarded the case for intuitionism as a wholly respectable option which he had consciously chosen and maintained consistently. Within this tradition, he had developed the integrating principles of his eclectic method: *viz.*, that theology is the interpretation of spiritual and

---

[17] That Malebranche had been read in the Holy Club we know from John Clayton's letter of Aug. 1, 1732 (see *Works* 25:331-34).Wesley recommended *The Search After Truth* in a letter to Samuel Furly, Feb. 18, 1756, and included it in the curriculum for Kingswood School; see another recommendation of it to Mary Bishop, Aug. 18, 1774. For competent reviews of Malebranche's epistemology, see Morris Ginsberg, *Dialogues on Metaphysics and on Religion by Nicholas Malebranche* (London, 1923), pp. 21-42; and also Gilson and Langan, *Modern Philosophy*, ch. 7. A critical analysis of the similarities and differences between Malebranche, Norris, and Wesley would be a very useful exercise. For Lucas's influence upon Wesley see Alexander Knox, 'Remarks. . . .' in Southey, 2:327-30.

[18] See Sermon 70, 'The Case of Reason Impartially Considered'; see also Sermons 10, 'The Witness of the Spirit', I', §I.12 and n., and 69, 'The Imperfection of Human Knowledge'.

[19] An *Essay Concerning Human Understanding* (1690), Bk. IV, ch. 17, §23. Locke distinguishes between assertions 'above, contrary, and according to reason': '(1) According to reason are such propositions whose truth we can discover by examining and tracing those ideas we have from sensation and reflection, and by natural deduction find to be true or probable; (2) Above reason are such propositions whose truth or probability we cannot by reason derive from these principles. . .'. For an example of an analytic discussion of (2), see *The Reasonableness of Christianity* (1695).

moral insights sparked by the prevenient action of the Holy Spirit, deposited in Holy Scripture, interpreted by the Christian tradition, reviewed by reason, and appropriated by personal experience.

From the same heritage came his understanding of an ascetical ethics, rooted in traditions of monasticism, finding its expression in a *contemptus mundi* that raises the human spirit above all inordinate attachments to 'this world'. After 1727 Wesley would come to understand this otherworldly view in richer detail—from à Kempis, Law, De Renty, Gregory Lopez, and many another; but he had already seen it much earlier, and at first hand, in the Puritan consciences of his parents and forebears. This rejection of 'the world' was less a loathing of God's good creation than a declaration of independence from bondages of worldliness and self-indulgence.[20]

This *asceticism-within-the-world* lay behind Wesley's moralism, and matched exactly his commitment to the great tradition of *ars moriendi*, 'the art of holy dying'.[21] This had been best described in English by Jeremy Taylor; a secularized version of it may be seen in Samuel Richardson's *Clarissa*.[22] It had then been sentimentalized and popularized by Edward Young's *Night Thoughts* (1742), Thomas Parnell's 'The Hermit' (1721), and James Hervey's *Meditations Among the Tombs* (1745-46). Wesley, for his part, scorned the sentimentality in these romanticized versions of otherworldliness. The Christian ideal in life and death, as he saw it, was equanimity and courage in the face of whatever providence might bring. And always the warrant for any such confidence was the God-given miracle of justifying faith and its assurance of grace. His notion, then, of holy living was a life emptied of spiritual pride but filled with the serenities of holiness —understood always as the Christian's love of God and neighbour.

Any such pluralistic method in theology was bound to generate tensions in Wesley's own mind and in those of his eager critics. It was neither neat nor clean-cut: the effort to gather and hold together so many disparate traditions was bound to strain the bonds of consistency—and all the more since Wesley was more interested in speaking to the needs of any given moment than in formulating a generalized view that might cover a multitude of conceivable instances.

From the earliest days of the Revival it appeared to half-friendly critics,

---

[20] He came to label this 'dissipation', defined as 'the uncentring of the soul from God'; see Sermon 79, 'On Dissipation'.

[21] See Beaty, *The Craft of Dying* (p. 29, n. 28, above).

[22] See Clarissa's dying words: 'God Almighty would not let me depend for comfort [i.e., strength] upon any but himself. . .', in *Clarissa, Or, the History of a Young Lady. . . .* (1747-48), Bk. 12, p. 92. One can take this novel as an important mirror to the eighteenth-century mind.

like Josiah Tucker and 'John Smith', that Wesley's attempts to integrate an evangelical soteriology (*sola fide*) with a catholic doctrine of grace had involved him in serious inconsistencies.[23] Later, Sir Richard Hill would repeat Tucker's complaint that Wesley's theology was 'a medley of Calvinism, Arminianism, Montanism, Quakerism, Quietism—all thrown together. . .'.[24] The Moravians and, afterwards, their solifidian allies (men like James Relly and William Cudworth) would add the further charge of 'Pelagianism'. The Calvinists claimed to have found 'the superior of a convent of English Benedictine monks at Paris' who had judged Wesley's *Minute* of 1770 as even more synergistic than 'popery'.[25] Both John Hampson and Augustus Toplady, from opposite sides, charged Wesley with absurdities in his attempted reconciliations of sovereign grace and human agency.[26] Bishops Lavington and Warburton had joined this chorus of critics of Wesley's confusions.[27] Alexander Knox stood almost alone in his judgment that Wesley's later sermons were more balanced than those from his middle period.[28]

For his part, however, Wesley stoutly maintained that his teachings *were* consistent, and this poses a problem for those who would interpret his thought and its own special dynamics. One might better begin, perhaps, with the fact that his critics were accustomed to a notion of consistency defined as literal identity in successive formulations (*semper eadem*). Wesley's idea of identity had much more to do with constancy of intention and perspective in successive circumstances. His critics could point to altered formulations and to the inner tensions in Wesley's writings—from 'early' to 'middle' to 'late'. His basic shift in 1738 had prompted drastic alterations in his understanding of the order of salvation (from his early view of a progression from holy living to justifying faith to a direct reversal of that order). It was not very long, however, before he relaxed his original insistence on conscious assurance as an either/or sign of justification. During that same period he also shifted his ground on the point of 'the remains of sin' in believers (what the schoolmen and Luther had called the *fomes peccati*).[29]

---

[23] See above, p. 19, n. 35.

[24] *Logica Wesleiensis: Or the Farrago Double Distilled* (1773), p. 43.

[25] See Sir Richard Hill, *A Conversation. . .*, above, p. 13, n. 10.

[26] See Hampson's *Memoirs*, vol. 3, chs. 7–9, and Toplady's *Caveat. . . .* (see above, p. 13, n. 10).

[27] See above, p. 13, n. 11.

[28] See Southey, 2:293–360, one of the most probing of all the theological appraisals of Wesley by any of his own contemporaries, and one of the most unjustly neglected.

[29] Luther had spoken of the believer as *simul justus et peccator* ('justified and yet still a

There was no inconsistency, as he saw it, in tilting the balance of a theological argument now this way, now that, depending on whether he was facing the antinomians from their side or the moralists from theirs. What was consistent, certainly after 1738, was his unwearied effort to find a proper place in the new evangelical soteriology for his undiminished concern for holy living. His goal was an alternative to both of the older polarizations that had separated the notions of Christ's *imputed* righteousness in justification from an actual *imparted* righteousness. He was convinced that both aspects of righteousness belonged as concomitant fruits of grace in the one mystery of salvation—provided only that they were both understood as means to the still higher end of perfection in love.[30] Thus, he found himself adapting Thomas Boston's familiar scheme of the 'fourfold states' of the soul's progress in faith to a 'threefold' one ('natural', 'legal' and 'evangelical').[31] Note how he included Boston's category of 'eternal' so as to fit his own concept of 'evangelical': 'The natural man neither conquers [sin] nor fights [it]; the man under the law fights with sin but cannot conquer; the man under grace fights and conquers'.[32] In such terms he could speak of 'Christian perfection' as the *end* of the order of salvation, and yet could also speak of 'the repentance of believers'. He could, moreover, teach his people to 'go on to perfection' and to 'expect to be made perfect in love in this life' and still react strongly against all advocates of *guiltless* perfection.

All this, of course, was bound to strike all lovers of single-track traditions as the evidence of a muddled head. To Wesley, however, it was a way of talking about the Holy Spirit's freedom to work as he wills and as human wills respond. The root difference in these competing views of consistency and development in theological statements is in their radically different pneumatologies and, consequently, in their differing views of the nature and roles of theological discourse. The Calvinists denied flatly any validity to natural virtue; the deists (and not a few Anglicans) firmly asserted it.[33]

---

sinner'). This paradox followed from his doctrine of invincible concupiscence; *viz.*, that the *fomes peccati* remains in the believer as long as he is in the flesh. For a further discussion of Wesley's difficulties with this problem, see Sermons 13 and 14, *On Sin in Believers*, and *The Repentance of Believers* (and their introductory comments).

[30] See his analysis of the relation of faith to love as a means to an end, in Sermon 35, 'The Law Established through Faith, I', §II.1–6.

[31] See St. Augustine, *Enchiridion*, XXXI, ¶¶118–19; see also Thomas Boston, *Human Nature in its Fourfold State*.

[32] See Sermon 9, 'The Spirit of Bondage and of Adoption', §III.8.

[33] E.g., Francis Hutcheson, whom Wesley repeatedly criticized; see Hutcheson's *Inquiry into the Original of our Ideas of Beauty and Virtue* (1725) and his *Essay on the Nature and Conduct of the Passions and Affections with Illustrations Upon the Moral Sense* (1726), and see Sermon 12, 'The Witness of Our Own Spirit', §5 and n. For an Anglican spokesman, see

Wesley had struggled with this problem for a long time; it had surfaced first in his 1730 sermon on 'The Image of God'.[34] He could see the partial truths on both sides; he rejected their fierce disjunctions. His own conclusion looked beyond any of the views of Butler or Hutcheson or the Calvinists:

> For, allowing that all the souls of men are dead in sin by *nature*, this excuses none, seeing there is no man that is in a state of mere nature. There is no man, unless he has quenched the Spirit, that is wholly void of the grace of God. No man living is entirely destitute of what is vulgarly called 'natural conscience'. But this is not natural: it is more properly termed 'preventing grace' [i.e., the grace of the Holy Spirit]. Every man has a greater or less measure of this, which waiteth not for the call of man.[35]

On another point, the Calvinists insisted on the radical depravity of all men, including the justified. Moralists like John Taylor of Norwich vigorously denied this.[36] Wesley's formal doctrine of original sin is stark, and yet he carefully nuances it with his rejection of invincible concupiscence and his emphasis on salvation as the restoration of the image of God (disabled but not destroyed by sin).[37] He could, therefore, deny the classical Protestant doctrine that all the good works of the unjustified are merely 'splendid sins'.[38] For if the Holy Spirit is God's personal agency of grace in the human heart, it is then possible in principle that the power of that grace might overcome the satanic power of sin and death, so that from being under bondage of not being able not to sin, a Christian might be endued, by grace, with the power not to sin wilfully—which is all Wesley ever really claimed for his doctrine of perfection.

From their side, however, the Lutherans and Calvinists were bound to read Wesley as teaching a doctrine of 'sinless perfection', and it is true that they could find enough occasional passages to stir their suspicions.[39] They

---

Joseph Butler's 'Dissertation Upon the Nature of Virtue', an appendix to *The Analogy of Religion* (1736), Bk. I, ch. 3; see also W. R. Matthews's edition of Butler's *Fifteen Sermons Preached at the Rolls Chapel* (London, 1967), Sermons 1-4.

[34] See Sermon 141, 'The Image of God.'

[35] See Sermon 85, 'On Working Out Our Own Salvation', §III.4; this late sermon is Wesley's most nearly complete statement of his own third alternative to the Calvinist and moralist extremes.

[36] As in *The Scripture Doctrine of Original Sin: Proposed to Free and Candid Examination* (1740), the enlarged 3rd edition of which brought forth Wesley's *Doctrine of Original Sin* (1757).

[37] See Sermon 44, *Original Sin.*

[38] For Wesley's rejection of the idea of 'splendid sins', see Sermon 99, *The Reward of Righteousness*, §I.4 and n.

[39] As in the 'standard sermon' Sermon 40, *Christian Perfection*, §II.4-24. It should also

could see inherent confusion in any effort to keep the distinction between voluntary and involuntary sins clear cut; they had long since swept away all Roman Catholic distinctions between mortal and venial sins. Thus, perfection as they could envisage it was eschatological, 'in the state of glory only'.[40] It was bound to seem to them that anything else ignored the full weight of sin and could serve only as a temptation to spiritual pride.

Wesley himself was always quick to correct any such interpretation of his doctrine of perfection by the antinomians (Maxfield, Bell, Cudworth). He was aware of the fatal dangers of self-righteousness, and gave voice to it in a lively little pamphlet, *Cautions and Directions, Given to the Greatest Professors* [of Perfection] *in the Methodist Societies* (1762). It is a sharp warning against pride, against 'that daughter of pride, *enthusiasm*', against 'antinomianism', and 'of *desiring* anything but God'.[41] He could speak as sensitively as any other Protestant of 'repentance in believers', since he understood that as we grow in grace, we grow in self-knowledge (*viz.*, true repentance); but he always stressed that repentance was also the work of the Holy Spirit and not a merely human act of remorse.

Between the 'early' and the 'mature' Wesley there is a great gulf fixed, by the transformations of 1738 and thereafter. The developments from the 'mature' Wesley to the 'late' are not so clearly marked. They are, however, considerable and important, and this is why the 'late Wesley' deserves so much more study than he has ever had. Even so, those developments that we can see did not constitute 'inconsistencies', in his eyes. Rather, as far as his intentions went, they express his unfolding understanding of the paradoxes of Christian insight. He scorned obscurantism in thought and rhetoric, but he took it for granted that the same truth spoken in love required different formulations in different circumstances. He was capable of short flights of speculation,[42] but he never supposed that the data of revelation could be conceptualized into a single system of coherent thought without ambiguous remainders. As long as he felt that a given formulation was in accordance with the general sense of Scripture and the winnowed wisdom

---

be noted that many of Wesley's followers also understood his doctrine as implying 'sinless perfection'; see John L. Peters, *Christian Perfection and American Methodism* (New York, 1956).

[40] See *The Westminster Confession*, ix.5: 'The will of man is made perfectly and immutably free to [do] the good alone, in the state of glory only (*non nisi in statu gloriae*)'; see also xiii.1.

[41] §§II, IV.

[42] As in his sermons 'On Eternity' and *On the Trinity* (Sermons 54 and 55); note, however, his methodological distinction between the mysteries of revelation and all reductive rationalisms.

of tradition, he believed that it was internally consistent with other formulations conceived in the same spirit. And this came from his conviction that it was the Holy Spirit who was leading all faithful Christians into all truth, even if not into identical formulations of it. Between 'The Circumcision of the Heart' and 'On the Wedding Garment' lie six lively decades of theological development. And yet, when they are read together, these two descriptions of the Christian life do not differ on any essential point. *That* is what Wesley meant by consistency.

5. WESLEY AND HIS SOURCES

It is clear enough that Wesley never expected to be edited critically; it is even probable that he would have deplored such an exercise as pedantic.[1] His quotations are rarely exact and rarely identified; his allusions are casual and his borrowings acknowledged vaguely or not at all. His sermons were for his 'plain people', but he could also be casual with his citations before a university audience.[2] His editors, by and large, have been content to reprint Wesley's texts as they stood in whatever edition they preferred.[3] The concern of the Bicentennial Edition of the *Sermons* to reopen some of the critical questions posed by Wesley's texts *and* his use of sources may very well be tinged with a hubris of its own.

And yet it is a fact that Wesley was working against an immense background with a remarkable repertory. The core of his learning was basically sound and his use of sources is usually apt. The value of tracing them out lies in their contribution to a composite portrait of Wesley as a folk-theologian. It suggests a view of Wesley as a technically competent theologian with a remarkable power of creative simplification, a revivalist who took special pains to conceal his erudition in the interest of the edification of his particular audiences. If this meant oversimplification, he was well content.[4]

---

[1] His own view of the Christian's priorities is reflected in the exhortations he drew up for his 'Helpers': 'You have nothing to do but to save souls'; 'never be triflingly employed; . . . neither spend any more time at any place than is strictly necessary' ('Twelve Rules of a Helper', #11 and #1, in 'Large *Minutes*'). He also has a snide comment on William Derham's preoccupation with the classification of butterflies in County Essex when his first duty was the cure of souls in his parish in Upminster; see Sermon 78, 'Spiritual Idolatry', §I.14.

[2] E.g., in his sermons on 'Hypocrisy in Oxford' (Sermons 150–51) he misquotes the 'Statutes of the University' to men who either knew them from memory or could readily have checked the texts.

[3] A partial exception here was the Canadian scholar, Nathaniel Burwash, *Wesley's Doctrinal Standards . . . Introductions, Analysis, and Notes* (Toronto, 1909); this follows Thomas Jackson's order for the first 'fifty-two standard sermons', but is addressed almost exclusively to the quasi-legal functions of the sermons in Methodist theology. A more fully annotated edition was published in 1921 by an Australian Methodist, E. H. Sugden (see above, p. 12, n. 6) but, again, Sugden's interest was focused on the legal status of the 'mature Wesley's sermons (the others are quietly ignored) and his annotations are largely for Methodist eyes only. Since Jackson's time, no new edition of the sermon corpus has appeared.

[4] In his Preface (1746), §4: 'My design is in some sense to forget all that ever I have read in my life. I mean to speak, in the general, as if I had never read one author, ancient or

The untoward outcome of all this, however, is that Wesley's success at concealment has actually encouraged both his disciples and his critics to ignore the intricate mosaic that lies behind his plain-style prose. The result has been a general underestimation of Wesley's actual stature as a theologian and, therefore, of his place in the transition from Protestant orthodoxy to 'modernity', and of his relevance in later ages. Yet another unfortunate side-effect of this has been the denominationalization of Wesley studies, with no more than a handful of exceptions.[5]

This means, therefore, that the task of source-tracings in the Wesley corpus is still closer to its bare beginnings than one might wish, and it is both a formidable and frustrating business. The data are insufficient, the clues too meagre, the methods thus far developed too haphazard. Yet even such a beginning as is represented here may set out the thesis (requiring further study for its verification) that Wesley lived and worked in a plurality of cultural worlds with little self-consciousness about their pluralism and with next to no distraction from his chief business as the spiritual director of the Methodist Revival. In retrospect, however, this 'plurality of worlds' can be identified with some clarity. There was, of course, the biblical world, but there was the classical world as well, in which Wesley shared a citizenship along with all the other cultivated people of his age. Beyond these, however, he also felt at home in the world of historic Christianity, especially in the patristic age, but in its medieval extensions also. Interestingly enough, his knowledge of the continental Reformation and the so-called Counter Reformation did not reach far past the commonplaces of seven-

---

modern (always excepting the inspired). I am persuaded that . . . this may be a means of enabling me more clearly to express the sentiments of my heart, . . . without entangling myself with [the thoughts] of other men.'

Note the echoes here and elsewhere from William Perkins, *The Art of Prophesying*, ch. 10: 'Human wisdom must be concealed, whether it be in the matter of the sermon or in the setting forth of the words. . . .'

[5] Southey's *Wesley* is still one of the few produced by an eminent literary figure, but he was scarcely able to estimate Wesley's theological background, even if he had been interested in it. Alexander Knox understood it much better and appreciated it much more; see above, p. 70. In later times both Maximin Piette, *John Wesley in the Evolution of Protestantism* (New York, 1937), and John Murray Todd, *John Wesley and the Catholic Church* (London, 1958), have recognized the Catholic elements in Wesley's heritage. Martin Schmidt's massive theological biography is excellent as far as it goes, but it scarcely glances at the final third of Wesley's career: see *John Wesley: A Theological Biography*, 2 vols. in 3 (Nashville, 1963, 1972, 1973). A promising sample of what it would mean for Wesley to be studied in an ecumenical context may be seen in Kenneth Rowe, ed., *The Place of Wesley in the Christian Tradition*. By and large, however, the agenda in Wesley studies has been of, by, and for Methodists, and their implicit claims to a proprietary right has been too readily conceded to them by non-Methodists.

teenth and eighteenth-century church history. When we come to British Christianity, however, and its tangled history of controversy and polarization, his resources are truly remarkable: here is much grist for well-furnished experts.

But Wesley's 'worlds' were not all 'theological'. He had read enough English literature to use it freely and to form quite confident value-judgments about it that dissented from the fashions of his time and those of ours as well. Moreover, he was widely and well read in most aspects of the intellectual, cultural (and industrial and economic) transitions of his century, and was able to bring much of this to his task as tutor to the uninstructed folk in his societies.

The attempted recovery of this complex array of sources is, therefore, much more than an exercise in historical curiosity. It displays Wesley in new dimensions; it makes it possible to read between his lines; it helps make sense of his eclectic aims and method; it illuminates his theological options at a level beyond his bare texts. The richer one's knowledge of this half-hidden mosaic, the more nearly full-orbed one's view of Wesley's mind and heart might be.

Holy Scripture

It would be redundant to say more about Wesley's self-understanding as a biblical theologian. A few added comments on his actual use of Scripture might, however, be in order. He knew it so nearly by heart that even his natural speech is biblical.[6] Unsurprisingly, judging by the texts from which he preached, the Gospel according to St. Matthew was his favourite book (1362 recorded usages); this, however, is followed by Hebrews (965), John (870), Luke (853), and 1 Cor. (779). His Old Testament favourite, again

---

[6] Many of his sentences are deft fusions of the biblical language and his own. For samplings of complete paragraphs that have more biblical texts in them than Wesley's own words and that still read quite smoothly, see Sermons 4, *Scriptural Christianity*, §IV.9; 22, 'Sermon on the Mount, II', §III.18; 44, *Original Sin*, §4; and 107, 'On God's Vineyard', §I.9.

From 1738 Wesley had Alexander Cruden's *Concordance*, which he speaks of as 'undoubtedly the best which hath yet been published in the English tongue'. In 1760 he published a very brief concordance (ten sheets) by John Fisher, one of his own preachers. In 1782 he published an abridgement of Cruden's 3rd edition by another of his preachers, Thomas Taylor. In addition to Cruden, he had access to some seventeen New Testament concordances, from John Marbeck (1550) to Matthew Pilkington (1749). The most popular of these was John Downame's (1630) which went through numerous edns. By middle life, however, he had become a walking concordance himself; see, e.g., Sermon 75, 'On Schism', §I.9 and n.

unsurprisingly, was Isaiah (668 citations), followed by the Psalms (624) and Jeremiah (208). His favourite New Testament preaching text was Mark 1:15 (190 usages), followed by 2 Cor. 8:9 (167), Eph. 2:8 (133), Gal. 6:14 (129), and Matt.16:26 (117). His favourite sermon text in the Old Testament was Isa. 55:7 (112 usages); this was followed by Jer. 8:22 (102), Isa. 55:6 (90),[7] Hos. 14:4 (87 times) and Ps. 147:3 (72 times). He could find the gospel even in the Wisdom literature, as in Eccles. 9:10 (55 times), and Prov. 3:17 (36 times). There are six books in the Old Testament from which he never preached: Ezra, Esther, Song of Solomon, Obadiah, Nahum, and Zephaniah. And while he seems never to have taken an apocryphal text for a sermon, his citations from the Apocrypha are frequent enough (e.g., from the Wisdom of Solomon) to suggest that his notion of the canon was more 'catholic' than 'protestant'.[8] In any case, it is clear that Wesley's sense of Scripture was organic and integrated.

His mastery of the *koine* Greek was thorough enough so that he read the New Testament in the Erasmian *textus receptus* for both devotion and study. He was, in fact, self-confident enough about his linguistic prowess that he could strike out on his own with independent translations and exegeses.[9] His knowledge of Hebrew seems to have been nominal,[10] but his interest in the medieval rabbinical commentators is more detailed than that of most of his contemporaries.[11] As for the Bible in English, his enthusiasm for the Authorized Version of 1611[12] (which he spoke of as 'our recent translation') was never better than lukewarm. But since it was so familiar and readily accessible, he used it more often than any other, and encouraged its use among his people. But he knew the other English translations also;[13] we are reminded of his rectory upbringing by the fact that when he quotes a Psalm, it is almost invariably from the Psalter of the Book of Common Prayer (which is also to say from the 'Great Bible' of

---

[7] If the texts in Isaiah 55:6–7 are combined, the total comes to 202.

[8] See Sermon 41, *Wandering Thoughts*, §II.3 and n.

[9] E.g., his *Notes*, and Sermon 16, 'The Means of Grace', §III.17.

[10] See Sermons 25, 'Sermon on the Mount, V', §IV.2; and 26 'Sermon on the Mount, VI', §III.7.

[11] See Sermon 36, 'The Law Established through Faith, II', §I.3 and n.; see also Sermon 66, 'The Signs of the Times', §I.2, where Wesley seems to know more than Matthew Poole about the medieval rabbinical interpretations of Gen. 49:10 (see Poole, *Annotations*).

[12] See Sermon 82, 'On Temptation', §I.l; see also Sermon 103, 'What is Man?', Ps. 8:3–4', §II.4: 'The new translation of the Psalms, that is bound up in our Bible, is perhaps more proper than the old, that which we have in the Common Prayer Book.'

[13] There was nothing in the eighteenth century to match Samuel Bagster's *The English Hexapla, Exhibiting the Six Important English Translations* (London, 1841), and yet Wesley seems to have had a competent working acquaintance with those same translations.

Coverdale of 1539). The Bicentennial Edition of his *Sermons* has attempted
a visual display in the footnotes of Wesley's way with Scripture. This may
deserve a special notice in the history of hermeneutics; at the very least it is
a demonstration that Wesley's claim to being *homo unius libri* cannot be
tested (or even fully understood) without close attention to the interactions
of the rhetoric of Scripture and the rhetoric and substance of his sermons.

The Classics

Wesley's biblical world was, however, no enclave. *Sola scriptura* was
never a displacement of, or substitute for, classical learning; and this was
natural enough in view of the fact that he had mastered the baseline curriculum of his Oxford education and had come to cherish the classical tradition as the font of Western civilization.[14] He was an accomplished Latinist
before he turned to theology as a special study;[15] his grounding in classical
Greek was at least adequate. Even as age wore on, he continued to quote

---

[14] Wesley's awareness of the bitter debates between the critics and advocates of the
classical curriculum in the seventeenth century is crucial; it explains his concern to set the
debate on a higher level; see Sermons 4, *Scriptural Christianity*, §IV.6 ('without love all
learning is but splendid ignorance'); 87, 'The Danger of Riches', §I.15; 109, *The Trouble
and Rest of Good Men*, §II.7; 146, 'The One Thing Needful', §III.1. But see also his *Address
to the Clergy* (1756), §I.3-6, *et passim*; see his letters to Dr. Thomas Rutherforth, Mar. 28,
1768 (§II.2, 10), and to Bishop Robert Lowth (London), Aug. 10, 1780. For the seven-
teenth-century debate, see the exchanges between William Dell (against classical curriculum),
as in *The Trial of the Spirits . . .* and *The Right Reformation of Learning . . .* (1653), and
Sydrach Simpson (for it) as in his Cambridge Commencement sermon of the same year.
See also Samuel How, *The Sufficiency of the Spirit's Teaching Without Humane Learning: Or,
A Treatise Tending to Prove Humane Learning to be No Help to the Spiritual Understanding of
the Word of God . . .* (1640). Christopher Hill has a lively and sympathetic summary of this
controversy in *The World Turned Upside Down* (New York, 1971), 241-46.

[15] This can be seen in the rhetorical sophistication of his Latin sermon, 'Hypocrisy in
Oxford' (Sermon 151); see also his transcription of an informal debate with Count Ludwig
von Zinzendorf in *JWJ*, Sept. 3, 1741. The style of the *sermon* is much more elevated than
that of the *debate*. Henry Moore must have had it from John Wesley himself when he
reported (*Life* 2:103): 'In the year 1731 the two brothers began the practice of conversing
together in Latin, whenever they were alone, chiefly with a view of acquiring a facility in ex-
pressing themselves in this language on all occasions with perspicuity, energy, and elegance.
This practice they continued for nearly sixty years; and with such success that if their style
did not equal, it certainly on some subjects approached nearer to the best model of conversation in the Augustan age than many of the learned have thought it possible to attain.'
See also Wesley's correspondence with Dr. Jan de Koker (a physician at Rotterdam), in *JWJ*,
June 14, 1738, and Nov. 10, 1749; see also *JWJ*, Aug. 10, 1738 (while at Herrnhut): 'I had
an opportunity of spending some hours with Christian David. . . . Most of his words I
understood well; if at any time I did not, one of the brethren who went with me explained
them in Latin.'

the classics without checking the originals; indeed, his later sermons are more ornamented with such tags than the earlier ones.[16] There is a charming vignette of Wesley in his old age in the memoirs of Madame Sophie de la Roche, a cultivated German noblewoman visiting England in 1786. She recalls having Mr. Wesley pointed out to her in the salon of the ship in which they both were sailing from Rotterdam to Harwich:

> Wesley sat and read Virgil, with spectacles, in an Elzevir edition. Heavens! I thought, if the Methodists' principles keep their sight as clear as that to the age of 83, then I wish I had been educated in their sect; for since their chief reads Virgil on the high seas, I too might have read my favourite works without damnation.[17]

His Methodist readers would scarcely have been impressed by more than the bare fact of Wesley's classical culture, but some of them would have been reassured by this evidence that his academic credentials were still in good standing. They were, however, more edified than they realized by this unadvertised alliance between sound learning and vital piety. In Wesley's own case this classical orientation was very much more than ostentation; it was an integral element in his theological perspective. He knew how deeply classical culture had shaped patristic Christianity.[18] He also knew how decisively, even in his own time, its rediscovery was reshaping the emergent Enlightenment in Europe. The Graeco-Roman legacy was a living resource for his Christian understanding, representing, as it did to him, an impressive demonstration of the grandeur and misery of 'pagan' culture at its best and worst. Some of the implications of this soteriological outlook become apparent in his exegesis—as, for example, his comments on Acts 14:15-17 ('the living God . . . who left not himself without witness . . .') and on Rom. 1:18-32 and elsewhere when he speaks of his conviction that God's providence has room in it for the salvation of 'heathens'.[19] Besides, he

---

[16] One of the indications that he was not relying on anthologies and florilegia is the fact that his quotations are so generally inexact. If he had been using something like, say, Herbert's *Jacula Prudentum*, one would have expected more exact copying.

[17] *Sophie in London, 1786*, Eng. tr. by Clare Williams (London, 1933), 78.

[18] One can imagine how delighted he would have been with C. N. Cochrane's *Christianity and Classical Culture* (London, 1944); one can also guess at some of his critical reservations.

[19] It was, indeed, the chief presupposition of his agreement with the old monastic epigram, *Qui facientes quod in se est*, which the nominalists also espoused and which Luther had denounced so violently. See Wesley's Oxford Diary, V, [vi]: 'Q. How steer between scrupulosity, as to particular instances of self-denial and self-indulgence? A. *Fac quod in te est, et Deus aderit bonae tuae voluntati.*' See also Sermons 85, 'On Working Out Our Own Salvation', §III.6-7; 66, 'The Signs of the Times', §II.10; 63, 'The General Spread of the

understood that a classical education tends to breed up in men and women a love of graceful speech and style; he had had good reason to appreciate this in his own family.[20]

In the sermons (and elsewhere, too) Wesley's favourite classical source was Horace; there are twenty-seven quotations from him in the sermons alone, some repeated in different contexts. One senses that he read Virgil with more personal pleasure, but he quotes from him only twenty-one times. Ovid follows with ten, Cicero with nine, Juvenal with seven. Thirteen others are quoted at least once: Aristophanes, Hadrian, Homer, Lucan, Lucretius, Persius, Pindar, Sophocles, Suetonius, Symmachus, Terence, Velleius Paterculus.

This display was more than mere ornamentation; within these borrowings we can find the germs of some of Wesley's most distinctive general ideas (e.g., his participation theme, his mind-body dualism, and his ideas about psycho-physical parallelism). These are major sources for his notions about human nature, human volition, and the human passions. Out of this heritage had come his predilection for form over raw feelings, his concept of conscience as a universal moral sense. Plato had bolstered his convictions about the ontological primacy of good over evil. The whole of the Graeco-Roman tradition had stressed coherence as a criterion of rationality. Besides, these ancient authors were shrewd critics of human folly; thus Wesley found in them discerning witnesses to the flaws in contemporary proposals about 'natural' theology and ethics. It was in this sense that his long dialogue with the ancients was a genuine *preparatio evangelica*; one might even suppose that he might still commend it as such.

Gospel', §9; 69, 'The Imperfection of Human Knowledge', §1; and 75, 'On Schism', §21.

See also, Heiko A. Oberman, *Harvest of Medieval Theology* (Cambridge, Mass., 1963), 129-45; Albert C. Outler, 'Methodism's Theological Heritage: A Study in Perspective', in *Methodism's Destiny in an Ecumenical Age*, Paul Minus, Jr., ed. (New York, 1969), 52-60; and Michael Hurley, 'Salvation Today and Wesley Today', in Kenneth E. Rowe, ed., *The Place of Wesley in the Christian Tradition*, 94-116.

[20] There was, however, an early outburst against classical learning in a letter to his brother Samuel (himself an instructor in classics at Westminster School), Oct. 15, 1735 (written aboard the *Simmonds* en route to Georgia): 'Elegance of style is not to be weighed against purity of heart; . . . Therefore whatever has any tendency to impair that purity is not to be tolerated. . . . But of this sort . . . are the most of the classics usually read in the great schools. . . . I beseech you, therefore, . . . that you banish all such poison from your school.' This was, of course, not a settled view; see the strong emphasis on classical studies in the curriculum of John's own school at Kingswood; see A. G. Ives, *Kingswood School in Wesley's Day and Since* (London, 1970), especially 1-106, and Appendix III, for the 'advanced course' and books placed by Wesley in the library at Kingswood.

Christian Antiquity

Wesley had a powerful sense of constancy within the turbulent experience of the Christian community through the centuries; this explains in part his lifelong interest in church history. He took it for granted and proceeded to re-enter the Christian past in order to appropriate its best treasures for his own time, because, amidst all historical change, he saw an essential continuity that had perdured. This, for him, was the essence of 'tradition'. He understood it as having been most clearly focused in the early centuries ('Christian antiquity'). Moreover, he believed it had developed in a more stable fashion within the Greek Orthodoxy than in the Latin West. His interest in patrology was more of a curiosity; his time at Oxford had coincided with the waning of one of its great epochs of patristic learning.[21] For all his life, thereafter, Wesley lived with these Fathers as mentors and contemporaries. In his baggage for Georgia he had included William Beveridge's ponderous folios of patristic texts (all eighteen pounds of them in their two volumes) and had used them as authorization for some of those unwelcome liturgical experiments that he tried on his ungrateful parishioners in Savannah.[22] But he learned much more from Eastern spirituality than liturgy. He found there a distinctive pneumatology which became the shaping force in all his later ideas about mysticism ('will-mysticism' versus 'unitive mysticism'). Here is the font of Wesley's most distinctive ideas about prevenient grace and human freedom and, most crucially, of his peculiar doctrine of perfection as *teliosis* (perfecting perfection) rather than *perfectus* (perfected perfection).

Early on, he was challenged to describe the ideal Christian, and did so under the ironic title, *The Character of a Methodist*.[23] What he had done, with no sense of incongruity, was to turn to the Seventh Book of the *Stromateis* of Clement of Alexandria, take its description of the 'true Gnostic',

---

[21] This epoch was signalized by the great edition of St. Cyprian's *Opera* by John Fell, Dean of Christ Church and afterwards Bishop of Oxford, and assisted by Henry Dodwell and John Pearson (1682; Eng. tr. by Nathaniel Marshall, Oxford, 1717), by William Beveridge's *Synodikon*, and by the pioneering work of Edward Pococke. It was true, as V. H. H. Green says in *The Young Mr. Wesley*, 33, 37, that scholarly interests in Oxford were in a general decline in the 1720s and 1730s, but this great tradition had not died, and Wesley is a useful case in point.

[22] See *JWJ*, Sept. 13–20, 1736; see also Mar. 5, 1736, Aug. 1736, for the 'List of Grievances presented by the Grand Jury for Savannah'. The first of these is that '. . . the said Rev. person . . . deviates from the principles and regulations of the Established Church . . . *Prima*, by inverting the order and method of the Liturgy. . .'. Then follow eleven specific allegations of such deviations.

[23] 1742 (*Works* 9:31–46).

and update it for the eighteenth century. His basic idea of the 'order of salvation'—as the process of the restoration of the image of God—is obviously an adaptation from St. Irenaeus's famous doctrine of *anakephalaiosis* (i.e., the recapitulatory work of Christ as the ground of all salvation). His central theme (divine-human participation) was learned in large part from Macarius, Gregory of Nyssa, and Ephrem Syrus.[24] His concept of Christian *koinonia* was more Greek than Latin, and this explains his freedom to correct what he regarded as the excessive sacerdotalism within the Anglican ecclesiology that he had inherited. At the center of all these ideas was his understanding of the person and work of the Holy Spirit as God's personal presence in the believer's heart and will, and in the Spirit-filled community and its sacraments. This enabled him to think of the Christian believer as indwelt and led by the Spirit within rather than being possessed by the Spirit as if by some irresistible force. He could, therefore, repudiate the charges of 'enthusiasm' brought against him, for he understood their mistaken assumptions as to what 'enthusiasm' really means.[25] Similarly, it was this Eastern Orthodoxy that helped save him from any temptation to the more conventional forms of 'unitive mysticism'.[26] Thus, just as he could refocus the will-mysticism of Scupoli, Scougal, and Bona, he also felt free to reinterpret the 'unitive mysticism' of such devout souls as Antoinette Bourignon, Madame Guyon, and De Renty.[27]

This distinctive view of the person and work of the Holy Spirit provides us with many a clue to aspects of Wesley's thought that are otherwise puzzling. Here, for example, is the source of his distinction between the irresistible sovereignty of God as *Creator* and the resistibility of the Spirit's prevenient action.[28] It is this pneumatology that lies at the heart of Wesley's

---

[24] See Outler, *John Wesley*, 9-15.

[25] See Sermon 37, 'The Nature of Enthusiasm'.

[26] Which he knew in the teachings of Eckhardt and Tauler and others. See also his criticism of Luther's *Commentary on Galatians* in *JWJ*, June 15, 1741: 'He [Luther] is deeply tinctured with *mysticism* throughout, and hence often fundamentally wrong. . . . How does he (almost in the words of Tauler) decry *reason* . . . , how blasphemously does he speak of *good works*. . . !'

[27] See Jean Orcibal, 'The Theological Originality of John Wesley. . .', 83-111 (see p. 45, n. 29 above). See also Robert Tuttle, *Wesley*, 218-27, 330-45; but see Evelyn Underhill, *Mysticism* (London, 1911), ch. 10. All of these have tended to deny the crucial distinction already made by W. R. Inge, *Christian Mysticism* (London, 1899), between the active and passive approaches to 'union'. Quite to the contrary, Wesley's own mysticism was self-consciously *dialectical*.

[28] A distinction already implicit in the canons of the Second Council of Orange (Arausiacum, 529); see Reinhold Seeberg, *Textbook of the History of Doctrines*, tr. by Charles E. Hay (Grand Rapids, 1954), 1:380-85. Wesley relies on it constantly; it is at the heart of the

visions of perfection; and it helps explain why his version of this doctrine was so readily misunderstood by persons long accustomed to the forensic orientations in Latin soteriology. In this older tradition, sanctification ('holiness', 'perfection in love') could be seen as the 'plerophory' (fullness) of faith. Thus also, the dominical command, 'Be ye perfect', could be seen as the covered promise that grace *can* triumph over sin. But the faith that generates holiness is itself a relationship that continues and grows in this life—in a dynamic process that is nuanced differently from any Latin concept of perfection as an achieved *state*. It was no accident, then, that Wesley regarded Montanus as having been misunderstood and maligned; he even thought that Pelagius had been slandered by St. Augustine.[29] His choice of Macarius's *Homilies* to stand in Volume 1 of the *Christian Library* (after the writings of Clement, Ignatius, and Polycarp) was symbolic; his references to St. Chrysostom, St. Cyprian, Tertullian, St. Athanasius suggest a long-standing familiarity. The result was that Wesley felt very much at home in 'Christian antiquity' and quite free to make full use of this resource in his own right.

From the Age of the Fathers to the English Reformation

Wesley's direct knowledge of church history from the fifth to the sixteenth centuries turns out to be no better than nominal. This may be explained partly by an Oxford curriculum which scarcely noticed the so-called Middle Ages; but there was also Wesley's conviction that the whole stretch of church history from what he regarded as the Constantinian 'Fall of the Church'[30] all the way to the sixteenth-century reformations had been a retrograde epoch at best. We have noted his debt to the popular piety of medieval England[31] and his conviction that the Edwardian *Homilies* were normative for Anglican doctrine.[32] We know also that he had read Thomas Fuller's vivid *Church History of Britain* (1656) along with Peter Heylyn's

---

notion of prevenience, but see his comments on *Thoughts Concerning the Origin of Power* (1772), his *Thoughts Upon Necessity* (1774), and the opening paragraphs of *Predestination Calmly Considered* (1752).

[29] See Sermon 68, 'The Wisdom of God's Counsels', §7; see also 'The Real Character of Montanus', *Arminian Magazine* 8 (1785):35–36. For a showcase of Wesley's patristic knowledge, see his open *Letter to the Reverend Dr. Conyers Middleton* (1749), especially §§3–12. For a critical analysis that tends to support Wesley's views on this point, see Robert Evans, *Pelagius: Inquiries and Reappraisals* (New York, 1968), chs. 5–6.

[30] See Sermon 61, 'The Mystery of Iniquity', §27 and n.

[31] See above, pp. 28–30.

[32] See above, p. 48.

Historia Quinquarticularis (1660). Both had helped confirm him in his preference for the Anglican tradition over any other.[33]

He was stoutly anti-Papist, and never changed his childhood conviction that Roman Catholics were still committed, on principle, to intolerance and to the subversion of English liberties.[34] In 1756 he published, without acknowledgement, his own abridement of Bishop John Williams's *A Roman Catechism, Together With a Reply Thereto*, and he knew both *The Canons of the Council of Trent* and also the *Catechism* published in that council's name by Pope Pius V.[35] What he may have known but not fully realized was that his own understanding of 'the *causes* of justification' tilted more toward the original proposals at Trent (Seripando, Contarini, Pole) than they did to those of the High Calvinists, especially on the crucial issue of justification's 'causes': *viz.*, whether Christ's atoning death was its formal or meritorious cause.[36] There is no record of Wesley's ever having read

---

[33] See Sermon 33, 'Sermon on the Mount, XIII', §III.1 ('so excellent a Church, reformed after the true Scripture model, blessed with the purest doctrine, the most primitive liturgy, the most apostolical form of government'); and his letter to Sir Harry Trelawney, Aug. 1780 ('Having had an opportunity of seeing several of the Churches abroad and having deeply considered the several sorts of Dissenters at home, I am fully convinced that our own Church, with all her blemishes, is nearer the scriptural plan than any other in Europe.') See also Sermon 13, *On Sin in Believers*, §I.3 and n., and below, pp. 94-95.

[34] See Sermon 127, 'On the Wedding Garment', §13 and n. Note Wesley's dictum in his letter to *The Public Advertiser*, Jan. 21, 1780: 'It is a Roman Catholic maxim, established not by private men but by a public Council, that "no faith is to be kept with heretics". . . . The members of that Church can give no reasonable security to any government of their allegiance or peaceable behaviour.' The Council in question was Constance (1414-18), where Jerome of Prague and Jan Hus had been burned for heresy despite safe-conducts issued them by the Emperor Sigismund. But this so-called maxim of Constance had been fixed upon it by its Protestant critics; there is no such statement (or inference) in the conciliar records themselves. Incidentally, this was the Council that deliberately refused to approve the doctrine of the moral right of 'tyrannicide' even by private citizens, as advocated by Johannes Parvus and Johan von Falkenberg. In view of the permission of reginacide in Pius V's excommunication of Elizabeth I (*Regnans in excelsis*, 1570), most English Protestants (and Wesley with them) were convinced that Roman Catholics were disloyal citizens, *ex professo*. This helps explain Wesley's passive complicity in the 'Gordon Riots' of 1778.

[35] There were numerous editions of the *Acta et Decreta* of the Council, from the first official edition of the complete set (Rome, 1564) to Wesley's time; the Bodleian had both the Antwerp edition (1694) and Cologne (1722), besides many earlier ones. The first Eng. tr. had been published in 1687. The *Catechism*, drafted under the guidance of Pius IV, was completed and published by his successor, Pius V; it was published even more widely and more often than the *Acta*. In addition, Wesley knew Paolo Sarpi's widely popular, but heavily tendentious, *History of the Council of Trent* (1619).

[36] The most credible account of the tragic process of the Tridentine debates has been provided by Hubert Jedin in three remarkable chs. in his *History of the Council of Trent* (London, 1961), vol. 2 (ch. 5, 'The Opening of the Debate on Justification'; ch. 7, 'The September Draft [1546]'; and ch. 8, 'Completion of the Decree on Justification'). All that

Bellarmine; we cannot tell how much better than common knowledge was his acquaintance with the famous *'De auxiliis'* controversy between the Dominicans and the Jesuits over grace and free will.[37] A direct comparison of Wesley's doctrine of justification with Bellarmine's *De Justificatione* (1601) is, therefore, all the more instructive, especially on the point of their shared view that justification effects both a relative and a real change in the believer.[38] Had he known it, he would have applauded the intention behind Philip Melanchthon's translation of the Augsburg Confession into Greek for the benefit of the Byzantines, where he chooses to translate *justificare* as *agiazesthai* rather than *dikaiousthai* (i.e., 'to make holy' rather than 'to make just').[39] In the same sermon in which Wesley finally came down firmly on the side of Christ's death as the meritorious, rather than formal, cause of our justification there is a sympathetic story about Bellarmine and his 'dying words'.[40] Bishop Lavington had been wrong in his invidious comparison of the Methodists and Papists;[41] what he had recognized, even if also distortedly, was a limited affinity between Wesley's soteriology and that held by the more moderate of the Roman Catholic reformers.[42]

Wesley could have known of the official transactions of Trent, however, was the final result in the *Acta et Decreta*, which was rigidly anti-Lutheran. Jedin shows how close the 'progressives' at Trent had come to a doctrine of justification by grace—i.e., by faith, hope, and love alone—but *without* antecedent merit. See Bellarmine, *De Controversiis* . . . (1601), 2:934-36, *'Explicantur causae justificatione'*; see also Wesley's 'A Disavowal of Persecuting Papists', *Arminian Magazine* 5 (1782):197-200.

[37] Precipitated by Luis de Molina's *Concordia liberi arbitrii cum gratiae donis* . . . (1588); in 1597 a *'Congregatio De Auxiliis'* was appointed by Clement VIII to adjudicate and settle the question. Their efforts continued, without success, till 1606. In 1609 the work was suspended by Paul V with a stipulation that no further discussions of 'efficacious grace' were to be published without express authorization by the Holy See.

[38] See Bellarmine, *'De Justificatione'*, I.ii, in *De Controversiis*; see also Sermon 43, *The Scripture Way of Salvation*, §I.4 and n.

[39] See Jaroslav Pelikan, *The Christian Tradition: A History of the Development of Christian Doctrine* (Chicago, 1974), 2:281.

[40] Sermon 20, *The Lord Our Righteousness*, §II.4.

[41] *The Enthusiasm of Methodists and Papists Compared*; see above, p. 13, n. 11.

[42] One may wonder how Wesley would have adjudged such a restatement of Roman Catholic views of justification as that of Hans Küng, *Justification: The Doctrine of Karl Barth and a Catholic Reflection* (New York, 1964), with its stress on *sola fide*; or, for that matter, how he would have appraised the 'secret histories' of Trent as now displayed in Jedin, *Council of Trent*, and John Dolan, *History of the Reformation: A Conciliatory Assessment* (New York, 1964). We know now, as Wesley could not have, that there were many reformers (Catholic and Protestant) who had already laid out the principles of grace and free will which he had then developed in ways not greatly different from his own.

The Anglican and Puritan Traditions

Wesley's clearest competence in church history, however, begins with seventeenth century Britain; his most vivid sense of personal involvement focused on the tragic conflicts between the Puritans and the Anglicans. Unsurprisingly, then, this period—from 'the Elizabethan Settlement' (1552-60) to the death of Queen Anne (1714)—provided him with his richest storehouse of sources. We have already seen how he tried to hold this unstable heritage in equilibrium with his pairings of Cranmer and Barnes.[43] In the Preface to the *Christian Library* he pays smug tribute to his national tradition: 'There is not in the world a more complete body of practical divinity than is now extant in the English tongue, in the writings of the last and the present century' (§1). Even a brief survey of Wesley's selections in that *Library* suggests an extraordinary range of reading together with a consistent editorial bias.[44] Later, in the *Arminian Magazine*, his horizons open out even more widely, always with an eye for suitable instructions for his own people and ammunition for their continuing skirmishes with the Calvinists.[45]

Wesley had been reading Anglican and Puritan divinity in Oxford, and maybe before. He knew the Anglican titans: Richard Hooker, Henry Hammond, Joseph Mede, George Bull, John Pearson, William Beveridge, John Tillotson. But he had a special fondness for the lesser lights whom we shall notice presently. He knew the great Puritans equally well: William Ames, William Perkins, John Davenant, Richard Baxter, John Goodwin, John Bunyan, Isaac Ambrose, Isaac Watts. Out of this jumble, and with his Eastern pneumatology as his key, Wesley had developed a soteriology which presents, as Professor John Deschner has rightly noticed, a 'new emphasis in Protestant theology up to his time'.[46] In this, therapeutic metaphors[47] tend to outweigh the forensic ones that had dominated Western traditions since Anselm. In this perspective it is the Holy Spirit who communicates all the graces of the Father and the Son, especially 'preventing grace': 'all the "drawings" of "the Father", the desires after God, which, if we yield to them, increase more and more; all that "light" wherewith the Son of God

---

[43] See above, p. 64, n. 2.

[44] See above, p. 36, n. 56.

[45] The editorial policy of the *Arminian Magazine* is accurately indicated by its first subtitle: *Consisting of Extracts and Original Treatises on Universal Redemption.* This would be altered in vol. 8 (1785) to 'consisting *chiefly* of. . .'.

[46] See *Wesley's Christology* (Dallas, 1960), 185.

[47] See, e.g., his emphasis on salvation as 'healing', as in Sermon 13, *On Sin in Believers*, §III.8 and n.; see also Sermon 17, 'The Circumcision of the Heart', §I.5.

"enlighteneth every one that cometh into the world". . . ; all the *convictions* which his Spirit . . . works in every child of man'.[48] This is why he was so strongly convinced that the much vaunted disjunction between the *imputed* righteousness of Christ (the ground of our justification) and his *imparted* righteousness (the Spirit's work in regeneration) posed a false alternative. The order of salvation, as Wesley had come to see it, is an organic continuum: conscience, conviction of sin, repentance, reconciliation, regeneration, sanctification, glorification. All of these are progressive stages in the divine design to restore the image of God in human selves and society.

Wesley's theology was elliptical in its form. Its double foci were the doctrines of justification and sanctification in a special correlation—two aspects of a single gracious intention, but separated along a continuum of both time and experience. The problem in justification was how Christ's sufficient merits may be imputed to the penitent believer as the righteous ground for God's unmerited mercy (i.e., the formal cause of justification).[49] And it was on this point of formal cause that Wesley parted from the Calvinists. They had stressed the Father's elective will, the prime link in 'a golden chain' of logic which led them link by link to the famous 'Five Points' of High Calvinism.[50] Wesley tilted the balance the other way because of his sense of the importance of the Holy Spirit's prevenient initiative in all the 'moments' of the *ordo salutis*. He could thus make room for human participation in reaction to the Spirit's activity and for human resistance as well—yet always in a very different sense from any Pelagian, or even 'Semi-Pelagian', doctrine of human initiative.[51] The result of this was an interesting distinction between efficacious grace in all but not for all. This pneumatocentric soteriology had still further corollaries. One was the distinction between 'wilful' sins ('mortal' sins in the Catholic vocabulary) and

---

[48] See Sermon 43, *The Scripture Way of Salvation*, §I.2.

[49] See Sermon 20, *The Lord Our Righteousness*, §II.9-12 and n. This issue of 'causality' was crucial for both Puritans and Wesley; see C. F. Allison, *The Rise of Moralism* (New York, 1966). The sticking point was that all theories of 'formal causality' entailed the notion of irresistible grace; Wesley's rejection of this was already implied in both his pneumatology and his doctrine of grace. This was grounded in the tradition established by Caesarius of Arles and the Second Council of Orange (520) to the effect that grace is an *infusio et operatio* of the Holy Spirit and is, therefore, in a profound mystery, resistible; see Seeberg, *History of Doctrines*, 1:380-82. On this question Bellarmine and Wesley had, in effect, agreed that everything turns on prevenient grace as a specific activity of the Holy Spirit.

[50] See William Perkins, *A Golden Chaine*. Match this with the nine Lambeth Articles (1595). Both of these statements antedate the Arminian controversy and the Synod of Dort. The 'Five Points' came to be listed in a familiar acronym, TULIP: Total depravity, Unconditional election, Limited atonement, Irresistible grace, and the Perseverance of the saints.

[51] See Seeberg, *History of Doctrines*, 1:375-85.

'sins of infirmity' or 'surprise' ('venial'). Another was the notion that assurance is never 'final' but may be forfeited by unrepented sins of any gravity, even venial ones.[52] A third corollary (Wesley's alternative to 'unconditional election') was a doctrine of covenant grace (echoing the famous covenant theology of Johannes Cocceius).[53] As a result, he could speak of 'the beautiful gradations of love' in faith's progress from its first assurance of God's pardoning grace all the way to its 'plerophory'.[54]

None of the elements in this special view of justification is original. But Wesley's assortment of sources for it is unprecedented—and so also is the way he compounded and simplified their convergent agreements. It includes a cluster of men who have long since dropped into undeserved oblivion: Hugh Binning, William Allen, John Rawlet, William Reeves, Thomas Grantham, John Plaifere, Samuel Harsnet, Valentine Nalson.[55] With all

---

[52] For Wesley's most extended comment on this point, see *Predestination Calmly Considered*, §§78–79; but see also Sermon 1, *Salvation by Faith*, §II.4 and n.

[53] Namely, the biblical idea of God and man in dynamic interrelationship of divine action and human reaction, as in Cocceius's *Summa doctrinae de Foedere et Testamento Dei* (1648; enlarged edition, 1654). See Sermon 6, 'The Righteousness of Faith', §1 and n.

[54] See Sermon 91, 'On Charity', §II.6: 'It is proper to observe here, first, what a beautiful gradation there is, each step rising above the other in the enumeration of those several things which some or other of those that are called Christians, and are usually accounted so, really believe will supply the absence of love. St. Paul begins at the lowest point, *talking well*, and advances step by step, every one rising higher than the preceding, till he comes to the highest of all. A step above eloquence is knowledge; faith is a step above this. Good works are a step above faith. And even above this, is suffering for righteousness' sake. Nothing is higher than this but Christian love—the love of our neighbour flowing from the love of God.' See also Wesley's letters to Arthur Keene, June 21, 1784, and to Thomas Olivers, Mar. 24, 1757.

[55] Binning was a brilliant Scottish theologian and preacher who had died young (1627–53); his ideas on justification, in *The Common Principles of the Christian Religion* (1659), *Several Sermons* (1660), and *The Sinner's Sanctuary* (1670), anticipate Wesley's by a century. William Allen was a 'General Baptist' who published *The Glass of Justification: Or the Work of Faith with Power* in 1658; he 'conformed' in 1662 and served as vicar of Bridgewater until his death in 1686. His phrase for 'the almost Christian' was 'the *negative* Christian', and his distinction between the faith of *adherence* and the faith of *confidence* is similar to Wesley's between 'adherence' and 'assurance'; so also are his ideas of prevenience (p. 27) and of 'faith working by love' (pp. 31 ff.). Allen's soteriology deserves a careful study in its own right. John Rawlet (1642–82) was a Cambridge trained popular preacher in the north; his influence on Wesley came through his *Christian Monitor, . . . An Earnest Exhortation to a Holy Dying* (1686), which went through twenty-five editions before the end of the seventeenth century and was constantly reissued throughout the eighteenth century. William Reeves (1667–1726) was another Cambridge trained patrologist (vicar of Reading), who reinforced Wesley's sense of the normative character of 'the undivided church'. Wesley had read his *Fourteen Sermons* in 1733 with evident approval. Thomas Grantham (1634–92) was a self-educated 'General Baptist' preacher in Lincolnshire whose habits of itinerancy and whose restorationist views in *Christianismus Primitivus* (1678) turn up, duly adapted, in Wesley—as

these men Wesley shared an Anglican orthodoxy older than Augsburg or Trent. But they, in turn, were scarcely more than a supporting cast for his main sources: Joseph Mede;[56] John Pearson, whose exposition of the section on 'the Holy Ghost' in his *Exposition of the Creed* (1659) was one of Wesley's most important sources;[57] Richard Baxter;[58] John Goodwin;[59]

---

well as his notion of justification by faith, *and love.* We have already noticed John Plaifere and the influence of his *Appello Evangelium* on Wesley (see above, p. 43). Samuel Harsnet (1561-1631) was a bellicose anti-Calvinist, a defender of Peter Baro against William Whitaker. The bulk of his writings was unpublished in Wesley's lifetime; but he had read Harsnet's famous anti-Puritan sermon preached at Paul's Cross in 1584. Valentine Nalson (1683-1723) was a popular Yorkshire preacher; Wesley had recommended his *Twenty Sermons* (1724, 1737) to his friends in their first 'Annual Conference' (MS Minutes, 1744, §84—June 29, Q. 14).

[56] Joseph Mede (1586-1638), Cambridge theologian whose main contribution to Wesley's thought came from his 'Discourses', in *The Works of the Pious and Profoundly Learned Joseph Mede* (published posthumously, 1677). In Discourse 26, pp. 113-15, there is a passage on justification and sanctification that Wesley could have written, and certainly subscribed to (e.g., p. 115: 'A saving and justifying faith is to believe [in Christ's merits] so as to embrace and lay hold upon Christ for that end, to apply ourselves unto him and rely upon him, that we may through him perform those works of obedience which God hath promised to reward with eternal life'). See Discourse 34 (p. 175) for a distinction 'between the Romanists and us' on *merit* and reward; see also Discourse 39 (pp. 213-15) on faith and good works. Mede's doctrine of repentance is developed in Discourses 38 and 62; his distinction between 'the fundamentals of salvation' and 'the fundamentals of ecclesiastical communion' (in a letter to Samuel Hartlib, Feb. 6, 1636) is one of Wesley's presuppositions in Sermon 39, 'Catholic Spirit'. See also Mede's *Clavis Apocalyptica* (1627).

[57] See 4th edition (1676), 327-30, and Wesley's quotations from Pearson in *A Farther Appeal,* Part I, §V.22-23 (*Works* 11:163-66). See also Wesley's lavish praise of Pearson in his letter to Cradock Glascott, May 13, 1764.

[58] Baxter's influence in Wesley's thought was decisive, and deserves far more careful and detailed study than it has had thus far. On this point especially see Baxter's remarkable retrospective of his own theological development and concerns placed at the end of Book I, Part I, of *Reliqiuae Baxterianae* (1696), 124-38: see also its abridgement in the *Autobiography of Richard Baxter* (Everyman's Library, 1931), 103-32.

[59] John Goodwin (1594?-1665), was a major Puritan source for Wesley's doctrine of justification, especially his *Imputatio Fidei* (1642). In 1765 Wesley extracted and published this as A Treatise on Justification, in connection with his controversies with James Hervey; this work he also included in his own collected *Works* (1771-74), vols. 22-23. Later he included an 'extract' of Goodwin's *Exposition of the Ninth Chapter of Romans* (1653) in *Arminian Magazine* 3 (1780), with the following prefatory 'advertisement': 'As many of my friends have long desired to see John Goodwin's *Exposition* . . . , and as the book is become so scarce that it is seldom to be found, I judge that [this extract] will be both acceptable and profitable to them.' Goodwin had been the Puritan vicar of St. Stephen's, in Coleman Street, London, a vigorous supporter of Parliament against the King and the Cavaliers and, later, a Nonconformist—still with a study in Coleman Street. He was, however, not a Calvinist in theology; indeed, he was denounced by the hyper-Calvinist, Thomas Edwards, as 'a monstrous sectary, a compound of Socinianism, Arminianism, antinomianism, independency, popery, yea and of scepticism, too'. It was Goodwin who was the real target of the

and even Isaac Ambrose.[60] It would be an important study in itself to re-view 'the history of justification' in the thought of this galaxy and to show by critical comparison Wesley's indebtedness to them and to the tradition in which they all stand.

We have already noticed that the deeper roots of Wesley's doctrine of perfection run back into the early Fathers; they had been supplemented by the ideas of such mavericks of the Spirit as William of St. Thierry and Thomas à Kempis. But there had also been a similar tradition in Britain that Wesley knew and had appropriated. Beyond his childhood acquaintance with Scougal, Wesley had also discovered (in Georgia) the *Memoirs of . . . Thomas Halyburton* (1715),[61] and then later James Garden's *Comparative Theology* (1700), one of the few works in Scotland directly inspired by Antoinette Bourignon.[62] Moreover, there was the decisive influence of Jeremy Taylor, whose works we have already noticed.[63] His personal acquaintance with William Law and their subsequent breach needs further detailed study; it began with undue veneration which then turned into uncharitable criticism as Law drifted more and more into the orbit of Jacob Boehme.[64] Wesley had also read the devotional works of Bishop Joseph Hall (1574-1656), and had learned from him how a Puritan soteriology and a Catholic spirit might be combined.[65] Even after the Revival was fully launched, he could claim encouragement from Bishop Edmund Gibson's explicit approval of his doctrine of perfection.[66] Wesley ignores the fact

---

pamphlet against 'the new Methodists' in *A War Among the Angels of the Church, Wherein is Shewed the Principles of the New Methodists in the Great Point of Justification* (1693).

[60] A Lancashire divine (1604-62/3) whose works were long held in esteem; Wesley devoted three of the fifty volumes of the *Christian Library* to Ambrose's writings.

[61] See Wesley's own *Abstract of the Life and Death of the Reverend Learned and Pious Mr. Tho. Halyburton* (1739).

[62] See the *DNB* entries on the brothers Garden—George and James. George, the younger and more eminent, was officially deposed from the ministry on account of his 'Bourignonism'; see his *Apology for M. Antonia Bourignon* (1699). The elder brother, James, was also deposed (1696) for his mysticism, and for his refusal to renew his signature to the Westminster Confession. Wesley thought well enough of James Garden's *Comparative Theology: Or the True and Solid Grounds of a Pure and Peaceable Theology* (1700) to extract and include it in his *Christian Library* 22:243-87.

[63] See above, p. 29, n. 28.

[64] See John B. Green, *John Wesley and William Law* (London, 1945), and Eric W. Baker, *A Herald of the Evangelical Revival* (London, 1948); see also A. Keith Walker, *William Law*.

[65] See Josiah Pratt's edition of *Select Works of Bishop Hall* (London, 1811), vol. 3, especially *A Holy Rapture . . . , Susurrium Cum Deo: Or, Holy Self-Conferences of the Devout Soul*, and *The Invisible World Discovered to Spiritual Eyes*. But see also vol. 1, and Hall's own accounts of his exertions on behalf of the *Via Media*, or *Way of Peace*.

[66] See *A Plain Account of Christian Perfection*, §12; see also the introductory comment to

that a great canonist and church historian like Gibson would have known the background of this controversy about holiness at least as well as he did.

But none of these men had ever envisaged any such goal as that of a Christian's 'being perfected in love' *in this life.*[67] Where had this provocative notion come from? Even a partial answer is curious. In 1741 Wesley had discovered An *Essay Toward the Amendment of the Last English Translation of the Bible* (1659) by an obscure seventeenth century exegete named Robert Gell. It is a huge quarto, a disorganized series of comments on the problems of biblical translation and the need for a revised version of the Authorized Version; and yet for all its bulk it does not begin to cover the whole of the canonical text. In an Appendix, however (pp. 785ff.), Gell had added a series of his own sermons on perfection as pure intention. In Sermon 20, 'Some Saints Not Without Sin for a Season', there is a vague reference to a then-recent controversy now so far forgotten that its full history may be beyond historical reconstruction. It concerns 'the condemnation' of Thomas Drayton and William Parker for their treatise, A *Revindication of the Possibility of a Total Mortification of Sin in This Life; and of the Saints' Perfect Obedience to the Law of God to be the Orthodox Protestant Doctrine* (1658).[68]

This 'succession' of Drayton, Parker, Gell on the doctrine of perfection was clearly a minority tradition and something of an elitist one in its way. Its main stress was on the triumphs of grace and on the power of a wholehearted love of God and neighbour to displace all other loves and so to overcome the remains of sin. What Wesley did—and this may have been his chief offence—was to universalize such an idea and, so to say, 'vulgarize' it. In this way he enlarged its scope, but also its risks of over-simplification on the one hand, and self-righteousness on the other. He was confounded and frustrated by the easy abuses thus invited, but was never deterred. And he was vindicated in that this doctrine became one of the hallmarks of the Methodist ethos; he could affirm with their agreement that 'the doctrine of

---

Sermon 40, *Christian Perfection.*

[67] See the questions that Wesley had from 1770 asked of his 'Helpers' before admitting them on trial into his 'Connexion': 'Every person proposed is then to be present, and each of them may be asked, "A.B., Have you faith in Christ? Are you going on to perfection? Do you expect to be perfected in love in this life? Are you groaning after it?". ' (Large *Minutes,* 1770, Q. 60. See also, letters to Samuel Bardsley, Feb. 1, 1775, and to Miss March, June 9, 1775.

[68] Their original *Vindication* has not survived; the *Revindication* is not listed in the catalogues of British Library or of Dr. Williams's Library, nor even in Donald Wing's *Short Title Catalogue of Books Printed . . . 1641-1700.* The only copy that I have ever seen is in the McAlpin Collection, Union Theological Seminary, New York.

Christian perfection' was one that 'God [had] peculiarly entrusted to the Methodists',[69] and had called them out as a separate movement in order 'to spread scriptural holiness over the land'.[70] Given his background in Eastern spirituality and his distinctive view of the office and work of the Holy Spirit, Wesley could never really understand why his optimistic views of the triumphant power of grace should offend so many Christians and confuse so many more.

On many points of churchmanship and polity that seemed crucial to the Anglican establishment, Wesley was almost blithely irregular. One may see this in the smugness of his report of his defiance of Bishop Butler's attempt to interdict him from irregular preaching in the diocese of Bristol.[71] On this point, as on so many others, he had simply been borne along by the actual circumstances of the Revival. What is more, he was willing to rest his case for his 'irregularities' on appeals to dubious 'authorties'.[72] Thus, on this score of practical ecclesiology, Wesley was less Anglican than on any other; his self-justification here was strictly pragmatic. The Revival had not

---

[69] See *JWJ*, Feb. 6, 1789.

[70] *Large Minutes*, 1789, Q. 3 (first added in 1763): 'What may we reasonably believe to be God's design in raising up the preachers called Methodists? A. Not to form any new sect, but to reform the nation, particularly the Church, and to spread spiritual holiness over the land.' See also Sermons 107, 'On God's Vineyard', §II.8; and 121, 'Prophets and Priests', §21.

[71] See above, pp. 26-28. For the text of a strikingly similar exchange between Wesley's grandfather (also named John) and an earlier Bishop of Bristol (Gilbert Ironside, the elder), see Edmund Calamy, *The Nonconformist's Memorial*, ed. Samuel Palmer, 2nd edition, 3 vols. (London, 1802-1803), 2:164-75 ('Whitchurch' in the section on 'Dorsetshire'); see Adam Clarke, *Memoirs of the Wesley Family* (London, 1823), 23-32. See also Glanville Davies, 'Evidence Against John Wesly [*sic*] (c. 1636-70)', in *WHS* 40 (1975):80-84.

[72] In a letter to James Clark, July 3, 1756, Wesley appeals to 'Dr. Stillingfleet's *Irenicon*' as authority for the essential equality of presbyterial and episcopal orders; he repeats this same appeal to the Earl of Dartmouth (Apr. 10, 1761), and finally to his brother Charles on June 8, 1780. Is it possible that Wesley did not know that Edward Stillingfleet (1635-99) had written his *Irenicum: or, A Weapon-Salve for the Churches' Wounds* in 1659 while still a struggling tutor (age twenty-four) and in the peculiar circumstances of the tragic need for 'comprehension' in the forthcoming Restoration? Was he unaware that Stillingfleet had subsequently repudiated his earlier position and had argued, in the Danby case, for the special jurisdictions of the Anglican bishops? Wesley's other chief authority for his thesis about the parity of presbyterial and episcopal orders was Peter King, *An Enquiry into the Constitution, Discipline, Unity, and Worship of the Primitive Church* (published anonymously in 1691 when King was still a Nonconformist and twenty-two years old); see Wesley's references to Lord King's 'Account of the Primitive Church' in *JWJ*, Jan. 20, 1746, and in his open letter to 'Our Brethren in America', Sept. 10, 1784 (§2). It is hard to imagine Wesley's not knowing that King had subsequently become an Anglican, the Baron of Ockham, Lord Chancellor of England, and had repudiated the ecclesiological views of his youthful *Enquiry* . . . ; this was common knowledge in Oxford and elsewhere.

only outlasted all precedent and expectations;[73] it had actually served the Christian cause in England and, therefore, the Church of England. On yet another ecclesiological frontier, he was convinced, before his time, that the core of Christian belief was more widely and more deeply shared by otherwise bitterly divided Christians than such antagonists had ever realized or were prepared to admit. He could, therefore, plead for and manifest what he labelled 'a catholic spirit'. He could also envisage a possible reunion of shattered Christendom, though less by any sort of 'conformity' to a single 'true church' than by some scheme of 'comprehension' such as had been proposed, prematurely, in the ill-fated Savoy Conference of 1661. And, despite his anti-Papist prejudices, he quietly rejected the 'conclusion' that Roman Catholics, as such, were beyond the Christian pale.[74] For all the bad blood the doctrine of predestination had stirred between the Calvinists and the Methodists, Wesley acknowledged it as an allowable 'opinion', if only it were not insisted upon as an essential dogma. He rejected Quaker and Baptist doctrines of 'the Spirit within' only in so far as it had hardened Christian folkways into divisive practices.[75] His open letter 'To a Roman Catholic' (1749) amounts to a basic agenda for a truly ecumenical dialogue.[76]

Wesley's critics charged that he was trying to have it both ways: justifying the perpetuation of separate traditions and yet also affirming the mutual recognition of a shared core and communion between them. And so he was; he believed that, beyond the polarizations that divided Christians into denominations, there continued a transcending *koinonia* into which they might all find their way back. Part of his theological mission was the discovery of such a *koinonia* that could stand equally and securely against sectarianism, on the one side, and secularism, on the other. This was the important premise behind his oft-quoted, oft-distorted, epigram that, on points not threatening essential truth, Methodists 'think and let think'.[77]

---

[73] See Sermon 63, 'The General Spread of the Gospel', §13 and n.

[74] See Sermon 74, 'Of the Church', §19, and his open letter of July 18, 1749.

[75] See his comments on the Quakers in *A Farther Appeal*, Part II, §III.5–10, and in Part III, §IV.7 (*Works* 11:254–60, 319); see also his letters of June 25, 1746, and July 10, 1747 (to 'John Smith'), and *JWJ*, July 6, 7, 12, 1739, Mar. 25, 1740, and Apr. 25, 1758. For the Baptists, see *A Farther Appeal*, Part II, §III.3–4 (*Works* 11:252–54), and *JWJ*, Aug. 10, 1739, Jan. 13, 1746, Apr. 3, 1751, and July 24, 1757.

[76] See Michael Hurley, ed., *John Wesley's Letter to a Roman Catholic* (Dublin, 1968), especially the introduction.

[77] See Sermon 7, 'The Way to the Kingdom', §I.6 and n. See also his letter to Mrs. Howton, Oct. 3, 1783: 'It is the glory of the people called Methodists that they condemn none for their opinions or modes of worship. They think and let think.' He had laid down the same principle, much earlier, in *The Character of a Methodist* (1742), §1: 'As to all

His practical efforts on behalf of this idea of 'comprehension' failed. He was an 'ecumenist' born out of due time, long before that term had been coined or the idea itself had evolved into its modern connotations. Even so, he never faltered in his hopes for a recovered Christian unity—and so he continues as an underdeveloped resource for any ecumenical vision that can conceive of that unity restored on other terms than abjuration and return.

And yet, for all this, he never understood himself as anything other than a staunch and loyal Anglican; he did not 'espouse any other principles . . . than those which are plainly contained in the Bible, as well as in the Homilies and Book of Common Prayer'.[78] We have already noticed his confidence that 'the Church of England is the most scriptural church in the world'.[79] The only points on which he quite deliberately deviated from the standing Anglican church order were: (1), open-air preaching (first begun aboard the *Simmonds* on Sunday, Oct. 19, 1735); (2), extempore prayers and preaching;[80] (3), the Methodist Societies as a connexion of persons acknowledging him as spiritual director; (4), the Conference as a conciliar alternative to any dependence upon episcopal authorization. For each of these irregularities he felt he had justifying precedents; besides, he had long since realized that there were no bishops able or even inclined to excommunicate him and his people.[81] Thus it was that he could see and interpret the breadth of the whole Christian tradition through Anglican spectacles but with wide-angled lenses. Even after his Deed of Declaration of 1784 and his ordinations for America, he continued to insist, sincerely, 'I live and die a member of the Church of England, and none who regard my judgment or advice will ever separate from it.'[82] He died in this vain hope.[83]

---

opinions which do not strike at the root of Christianity, we "think and let think".'

[78] Letter to *Lloyd's Evening Post*, Dec. 1, 1760; see also JWJ, Sept. 13, 1739: 'A serious clergyman desired to know in what points we differed from the Church of England. I answered: "To the best of my knowledge, in none. The doctrines we preach are the doctrines of the Church of England; indeed, the fundamental doctrines of the Church, clearly laid down, both in her Prayers, Articles, and Homilies".' See his final reiteration and his apology for his 'irregularities', JWJ, Apr. 12, 1789.

[79] See above, p. 102, n. 32.

[80] See above, p. 28.

[81] See Charles J Abbey, *The English Church and Its Bishops*, 2 vols. (London, 1887), 1:249-50, 353-55, 383-97; 2:92-93, 132-36, for the suggestion that episcopal disapproval of Wesley never amounted to a firm proposal to bring him under active ecclesiastical or civil discipline.

[82] 'Farther Thoughts on Separation from the Church', *Arminian Magazine* 13 (1790): 216. See also JWJ, Apr. 12 (Easter), 1789.

[83] See Frank Baker, *John Wesley and the Church of England*, 304-23; see also John

Contemporary Culture

Wesley's orientation toward the Christian past did not, however, divert his interest from his own world and his own time. The abandonment of his academic career and his identification with the masses did not assuage his voracious appetite for reading, even though much of that reading was in haste and on the run.[84] For the most part he sought out books that served his purposes as theological tutor to the Methodists, and yet it is equally clear that he was also driven by an unflagging intellectual curiosity that continued with him to the end.[85] He lived in an age of exploration; he read the reports of the great voyagers eagerly, with an interesting mixture of credulity and critical reserve.[86] He himself had long since lost his illusions about the myths of the 'noble savage' and the unspoiled 'children of nature', through his experiences with the native Americans in Georgia. He

---

Walsh, 'Methodism at the End of the Eighteenth Century', in Davies and Rupp, eds., *A History of the Methodist Church in Great Britain* 1:277–315.

[84] There was this much warrant for Ronald Knox's otherwise snide remark that Wesley was 'not a good advertisement for reading on horseback'; see *Enthusiasm* (Oxford, 1950), 447.

[85] In the last seven years of his life there are thirty-five *Journal* listings of recorded readings amidst incessant travel, preaching, and the care of the Societies. They range widely, from a quite new translation of 'Voltaire's *Memoirs*' (JWJ, Aug. 26, 1784: *Memoirs of the life of Voltaire . . . written by himself,* 1784) to 'LeVayer's Animadversions' (JWJ, June 8, 1785: Francois de la Mothe LeVayer, *Notitia Historicorum Selectorum . . . ,* 1678), to 'Perry's Treatise upon the Gravel and Stone,*' with a favourable comment on Perry's experimental use of 'lithontriptics' (JWJ, Nov. 3, 1785: *A Disquisition of the Stone and Gravel, with other Diseases of the Kidneys, Bladder, etc. 1777, . . . With Strictures on the Gout* added to 7th edition, 1785), to 'Dr. Withering's *Treatise on Foxglove*' (JWJ, Mar. 21, 1786: William Withering, 'the elder', *An Account of the Foxglove and some of its medical uses: with practical remarks on Dropsy,* 1785).

Toward the end he let others read to him, but his range is still wide; see diary, Jan. 12, 1791, when Elizabeth Ritchie 'read Mexico', re-read Lewis Stuckley, *A Gospel Glass . . .* (already extracted in the *Christian Library,* 33:5–269) and also Archibald Campbell, *The Doctrine of a Middle State between Death and the Resurrection* (1721).

His last reading was the poignant biography of an African ex-slave; see diary, Feb. 23, 1791; 'read *Gustavus Vasa'—viz.,* Olaudah Equiano, *The interesting narrative of the life of O. Equiano, or G. Vassa, the African . . . written by himself* (1789; 2nd edition, 1790). This influenced his famous 'last letter' to William Wilberforce in ardent support of the latter's anti-slavery struggles.

[86] See Thomas Salmon, *Modern History: Or the Present State of All Nations,* 3 vols. (1744–46); and Aubry de la Motraye, *Travels Through Europe, Asia, and Into Parts of Africa,* 3 vols. (1732). See also JWJ, Feb. 17, 1787, where Wesley says of Du Halde's *Description of China and Chinese Tartary,* '[His] word I will not take for a straw; but there are many and just remarks in the treatise, to which few impartial men would have any objection, in whatever form they were proposed.' In 1785 he read William Coxe's account of his *Travels into Poland, Russia, Sweden, and Denmark,* published just the previous year.

was, therefore, inclined to find in the various accounts of other native peoples (the Hottentots in South Africa and the Laplanders in arctic Europe)[87] still further confirmation of his belief that sin (in the sense of the wilful violation of acknowledged moral standards) is more nearly the universal norm than mere innocence or ignorance. But he was also certain that the *chief* hindrance to 'the general spread of the gospel' was the blatantly inhumane behaviour of nominal and pseudo-Christians at home and abroad.[88] Thus, he could hold on to his doctrines of universal redemption in Christ, and of the Holy Spirit's universal presence and prevenient activity among all peoples, and still denounce various Christian betrayals of the gosel.[89]

Given his providentialist views of history, he found in Edward Brerewood's demographic calculations that no more than 'five parts in thirty' of the world's population 'are as much as nominally Christian'[90] a further proof of the relative failure of Christian missions.[91] And yet he also took heart from various reports of new missionary ventures and revivals in other parts of the world. He looked ahead to the future expansion of Christianity with rising expectations.[92] His favourite sources here were such books as Jonathan Edwards's *Faithful Narrative* and John Gillies's *Historical Collections Relating to Remarkable Periods of the Success of the Gospel* (1754). Moreover, he thought he saw how these visions of a Christianized world could be fitted into the secularized doctrines of human progress newly advertised by men like George Hakewill and Bernard Le Bovier de Fontenelle.[93] Here, again, one sees his unfaltering confidence that his optimism of grace

---

[87] For Wesley's knowledge of the Hottentots and the Cape of Good Hope, see Sermon 28, 'Sermon on the Mount, VIII', §9 and n.; and for the Laplanders, Sermon 38, 'A Caution against Bigotry', §I.4 and n.

[88] See Sermon 63, 'The General Spread of the Gospel', §22 and n.

[89] For Wesley's view on universal redemption, see Michael Hurley, 'Salvation Today and Wesley Today', 101–12; see above, pp. 96–99.

[90] See his *Enquiries Touching the Diversities of Languages and Religions Through the Chief Parts of the Earth* (1614); see also Sermon 63, 'The General Spread of the Gospel', §2 and n.

[91] For Wesley's other references to Brerewood, see Sermon 15, *The Great Assize*, §II.4 and n.

[92] See Sermon 102, 'Of Former Times', intro. and n.

[93] See George Hakewill, *Apologie or Declaration of the Power and Providence of God in the Government of the World . . .* (1627, 1630, 1635); and Bernard Le Bovier de Fontenelle, *Dialogues of the Dead* (1st edition, in French, 1683; Eng. tr. by John Hughes, 1708), and *Conversations on the Plurality of Worlds* (1st edition in Fr., 1686; Eng. tr. by Mrs. Aphra Behn; four editions from 1688 to 1760); see Sermon 102, 'Of Former Times', §§20–23, and n. on §21.

could co-exist with emerging new ideas about the human condition and the human prospect.

Wesley was rationalist enough to realize that his theology had to be correlated with the scientific revolution of his time, and he was aware of some of the problems involved in this. He had grown up with the comfortable assurance that 'natural philosophy', when true, would always be in accord with the Christian vision of the wisdom of God in creation, which is to say, with the long tradition represented by such men as John Ray, William Derham, and the Boyle Lecturers.[94] He had read Bishop Thomas Sprat's *History of the Royal Society* (1667) and a rich bibliography of other samplings of 'the new science' besides.[95] But he was also aware of the waning of the older confidence that Christian theology could forever regard 'natural theology' as a 'handmaiden (*ancilla*) to theology' (herself *regina scientiarum*). 'The Age of Newton' had posed radical difficulties to all historical Christian world views and, most especially, to its doctrines of miracles and providence. Moreover, Wesley had more than an inkling of the drastic consequences for the *fides historica* in the scepticism of David Hume and the critical idealism of Immanuel Kant. In reaction, he sought out various critics of Newton and appealed to them, less in refutation of Newton's empirical findings than in support of his own views of the sovereignty of divine providence.[96] For a brief span he flirted with the bizarre anti-Newtonian hypotheses of John Hutchinson, to the effect that an entire and

---

[94] John Ray (1627-1705) was a theologian, natural scientist, and charter Fellow of the Royal Society; it was his *Wisdom of God Manifested in the Works of Creation* (1691; twelve editions by 1759) that Wesley took as a model; see Charles Raven's biography, *John Ray, Naturalist, His Life and Works* (Cambridge, 1942), see also *Organic Design, a Study of Scientific Thought from Ray to Paley* (London, 1954). William Derham (1657-1735), rector of Upminster (Essex) and a Fellow of the Royal Society; see his *Astro-Theology* (1715) and *Physico-Theology* (1716). The Boyle Lectures had been founded in 1692 by Robert Boyle with the general intent of confirming the then reigning religious consensus about the harmony between the new sciences and the old faith.

[95] For Wesley's interests in contemporary natural phenomena (earthquakes, volcanoes, electricity, astronomy), see Sermons 15, *The Great Assize*, and 55, *On the Trinity*, and nn. It may be mentioned here that he read everything on electricity he could lay hands on, and was especially interested in the controversial accounts of geological origins—as between Thomas Burnet, *The Sacred Theory of the Earth*, 2 vols. (1684, 1689), and William Whiston, *A New Theory of the Earth* (1696). What was at stake here was a theological interpretation of the creation stories of Genesis (and of the Flood); that Wesley's interest in these questions never flagged is suggested by his reading of Oliver Goldsmith's 8-vol. *History of the Earth and Animated Nature* (1774), sometime before 1789; see Sermon 130, 'On Living without God', §1.

[96] See Wesley's *Survey* (1777), 3:328: 'It will be easily observed that I do not deny but only doubt of the present [Newtonian] system of astronomy.' See Sermons 55, *On the Trinity*, §10 and n.; and 77, 'Spiritual Worship', §I.6 and n.

inspired cosmology had been encoded in the unpointed Hebrew of 'the first five books of Moses';[97] he quickly realized this as a false move and abandoned it.

He was, however, no mere critic. He gathered together what he regarded as the best in contemporary science and produced his own *Survey of the Wisdom of God in Creation: Or, A Compendium of Natural Philosophy.*[98] Largely borrowed (from good sources), it is an impressive collection, well-organized and open to the problems of integrating religion and science. Moreover, in the sermons (especially the later ones) we are casually confronted with what turn out to be competent references to the new astronomy (planetary distances, comets and 'fixed stars', the speed of light, and 'the plurality of worlds'). Wesley was the first popular theologian to recognize the importance of the newly discovered phenomenon of electricity[99] (relating it to his own prescientific notions of 'ethereal fire'). Indeed, he became a pioneer in the therapeutic uses of mild electrical shock, installing 'electrification machines' in his paramedical clinics in London and Bristol.[100]

Just as he struggled with the challenges to faith from natural philosophy, so also he sought to defend his people from the secularization of morality, which he recognized in all theories of intrinsic human virtue in their beginnings, as he reckoned them, in Shaftesbury, the deists, and even in Joseph Butler.[101] We have noted how this polemic against 'intrinsic virtue' was matched by his violent alarm over the spread of the economic theories of

---

[97] See Hutchinson, *Moses' Principia* (1724); see also Sermons 77, 'Spiritual Worship', §I.6 and n., and 69, 'The Imperfection of Human Knowledge', §I.5 and n.; see also Charles Singer, *A Short History of Scientific Ideas to 1900* (New York, 1959), ch. 8.

[98] First in two volumes (1763), then in three (1770), and finally in five (1777).

[99] See Sermon 15, *The Great Assize*, §III.4 and n.

[100] See JWJ, Nov. 9, 1756: 'Having procured an apparatus on purpose, I ordered several persons to be electrified who were ill of various disorders; some of whom found an immediate, some a gradual, cure. From this time I appointed, first some hours in every week, and afterward an hour in every day, wherein any that desired it might try the virtue of this surprising medicine. Two or three years after, our patients were so numerous that we were obliged to divide them; so part were electrified in Southwark, part at the Foundery, others near St. Paul's, and the rest near the Seven Dials.' See also Nov. 16, 1747.

Few of Wesley's people could afford the services of physicians; he, therefore, sought to supply them with what he could, including a manual of *Primitive Physick: Or, an Easy and Natural Method of Curing Most Diseases* (1747, and twenty-two more editions by 1791). It is no more than a sample of medical *curiosa* today; yet it does manage to enforce Wesley's point that health is *wholeness*—and 'natural'.

[101] See his long running battle with Francis Hutcheson after the latter's publication of *An Inquiry into the Original of Our Ideas of Beauty and Virtue* (1725) and his *Essay on the Nature and Conduct of the Passions* . . . (1726). See above, p. 71, n. 33.

laissez-faire that finally found a classic statement in Adam Smith's *Wealth of Nations* (1776). What offended Wesley here was the thesis that surplus accumulation was, in fact, the very foundation of economic well-being. In flat contradiction, Wesley insisted that all surplus accumulation was mortal sin.[102] He was, of course, swimming against a massive current, and made scant headway. His people were prepared to follow his first two rules for 'the use of money': *viz.*, 'gain all you can honestly' and 'save all you can carefully'. But the third rule ('give all you can—namely, all you have over and above necessities and conveniences') was asking too much—then, or since.

Wesley's father before him had been something of a marginal figure in the literary world as contributor to *The Athenian Mercury*, *The Athenian Oracle*, and *The Athenian Gazette*.[103] On his own, he had produced a poetic *Life of Our Blessed Lord* (1693) and some very ambitious *Dissertations on the Book of Job* (1735).[104] Young John had grown up in the literary climate of *The Spectator*, *The Tatler*, and *The Guardian*; one suspects that he was always an essayist at heart. For all his notoriety as an 'enthusiast', he maintained a mutually admiring friendship with Dr. Samuel Johnson, the ruling 'Grand Cham' of eighteenth-century letters.[105] Thus, behind the conventional stereotype of the itinerant evangelist there was a man of letters whose literary lore and exacting tastes are discernible 'between his lines'. In the sermons there are echoes from English literature from Bede to Chaucer, to Dryden, to Pope, to Thomson. He found Milton more profound than Shakespeare, and, by the same criterion, he adjudged both Edward Young and Matthew Prior as major poets.[106] His appraisals of Alexander Pope were mixed, but he was familiar enough with his poetry to paraphrase it

---

[102] See Sermon 50, 'The Use of Money', especially introduction; see also Sermons 28, 'Sermon on the Mount, VIII'; 87, 'The Danger of Riches'; 108, 'On Riches'; and 131, 'The Danger of Increasing Riches'.

[103] In association with their eccentric editor, John Dunton, who was also the elder Wesley's brother-in-law.

[104] See also his *History of the Old and New Testament Attempted in Verse*, 3 vols. (1704).

[105] This was shared by his brother Charles and also their sister, Martha Hall. See Moore, 2:253-55, for a summary of Johnson's comments on Wesley, and *JWJ*, Dec. 18, 1783, for a report of his last visit 'with that great man, Dr. Johnson, who is sinking into the grave by a gentle decay' (Johnson was then 74, Wesley 80). There are at least seven references to Wesley (all sympathetic) in James Boswell's *Life of Johnson* (3rd edition, 1799).

[106] In a letter of Oct. 26, 1745, he speaks of Shakespeare as 'our heathen poet'; but he knew him well (especially *Hamlet*, *The Tempest*, and *Twelfth Night*). See Sermon 77, 'Spiritual Worship', §III.5, where Prior's *Solomon* is adjudged as 'one of the noblest poems in the English tongue'; in Sermon 92, 'On Zeal', §III.6, Edward Young is spoken of as 'our great poet'.

almost casually.[107] He knew Dryden fairly well but used him sparingly. He admired Dean Jonathan Swift's sermon 'On the Trinity', and shared Swift's disdain for English arrogance in Ireland.[108] He could not abide Laurence Sterne, Voltaire, or Lord Chesterfield.[109]

Wesley's 'plain people' knew well enough how sternly he denounced the English theatre in general as 'a sink of all profaneness and debauchery'.[110] What they can scarcely have realized was the range of Wesley's interest in English drama from the Restoration to his own day. There is a diary record for November 18, 1729, of his attending in London a performance of John Fletcher's *Scornful Lady*,[111] and there is ample evidence of his having read a great deal of English melodrama. In the corpus there are quotations from more than a score of plays.[112] In addition, we have records of his readings of other dramatic works by these same playwrights, not to mention various plays by at least another dozen dramatists from which he never quoted.[113]

An odd instance of this paradox may be seen in Sermon 44, *Original Sin*, §II.9; there a snatch of poetry that is very apt (but uncited) turns out to be a quotation from a once famous melodrama by a once famous dramatist,

---

[107] See Sermons 67, 'On Divine Providence', §19; 60, 'The General Deliverance', §III.5; and 78, 'Spiritual Idolatry', §II.2.

[108] See his *Short Method of Converting All the Roman Catholics in the Kingdom of Ireland* (1752).

[109] See Sermon 100, 'On Pleasing All Men', §I.5, where Sterne is identified as 'a late witty writer'; but in *JWJ*, Feb. 11, 1772, his comment on *A Sentimental Journey* (1768) is peremptory: 'Sentimental! What is that? It is not English. . . . It is not sense. . . . For oddity, uncouthness, and unlikeness to all the world beside, I suppose [Sterne] is without a rival.' In a letter to Richard Locke, Sept. 14, 1770, Wesley speaks of Voltaire as 'that wretched man'; see also Sermons 84, *The Important Question*, §III.11; and 120, 'The Unity of the Divine Being', §§19-20. For Wesley's comments on Chesterfield, see Sermons 100, 'On Pleasing All Men', §4 and n.; and 128, 'The Deceitfulness of the Human Heart', §II.7.

[110] See Sermons 89, 'The More Excellent Way', §V.4 and n.; and 94, 'On Family Religion', §III.14.

[111] See also, *JWJ*, Mar. 28, 1750, where Wesley records a meeting with 'the famous Mr. Griffith, of Carnarvonshire—a clumsy, overgrown, hard-faced man, whose countenance I could only compare to that (which I saw in Drury Lane thirty years ago) of one of the ruffians in *Macbeth*'. Wesley was seventeen in 1720 and a student at the Charterhouse.

[112] E.g., Joseph Addison, *Cato*; John Dryden, *The Conquest of Granada*; John Hughes, *The Siege of Damascus*; Nathaniel Lee, *Oedipus*; Thomas Otway, *The Orphan*; Nicholas Rowe, *Tamerlane*, *The Ambitious Step-mother*, *The Fair Penitent*; Shakespeare, *Hamlet*, *The Tempest*, *Twelfth Night*; Sophocles, *Ajax*; Terence, *The Eunuch*, *The Lady of Andros*, and *The Self-Tormentor*.

[113] E.g., Lord Lansdowne, John Dennis, Richard Taverner, Thomas Southerne, Ben Jonson, Charles Molloy, William Wycherley, George Etheridge, George Lillo, James Miller, George Ruggle, William Mountfort, and David Mallet.

Thomas Otway. The source is *The Orphan*, published and staged in 1680, first read by Wesley in May of 1726, now quoted in 1759. *The Orphan* was still being performed in the eighteenth century, but would a quotation from it be readily recognizable by Wesley's readers? And whence would Wesley have retrieved it? Another interesting sample of this literary outreach—the longest quotation still, alas, unidentified—is a passage of eight lines in Sermon 67, 'On Divine Providence', §19. Obviously, it was familiar enough to Wesley; it neatly ornaments his argument. One might think it would be equally obvious to at least some others; yet none of many probes has found its source. These illustrations of Wesley's casual recourse to his literary heritage make two important points: the heritage enriched his rhetoric, and yet he makes no show of it whatever. This was his way of heeding Ovid's counsel about the artistry of concealing one's art.[114]

The Revival's greatest literary influence, however, came from its hymnody. This is the common witness of all the reports we have from the Methodists and from others. The brothers Wesley set great store by the fact that their people *sang* the same doctrine in their hymns as they heard and read in their sermons. Accordingly, the most copious source of quotations in the written sermons, besides the Scripture itself, is from the succession of hymn collections provided for the Methodist people. Here, Charles's contribution to the Revival was unique;[115] far more of his hymns have been sung by more Christians (and not just Methodists alone) than any sermon of John's has ever been read. And yet, John's hymnody reached beyond his brother's poetry. In the quasi-official *Collection of Hymns for the Use of the People Called Methodists* of 1780 there are hymns by Isaac Watts, along with a small sheaf of excellent translations by John himself of great Lutheran hymns from the Reformation's first century.[116] As with so much else, Wesley had very definite notions as to the role of hymns and singing in the Methodist services; these were summed up in his *Directions for congregational singing*, which appeared as an appendix to *Select Hymns: With Tunes Annext* in 1761.[117] Just as he scorned the ornate style in

---

[114] See letter to Samuel Furly, July 15, 1764.

[115] See Frank Baker, *Representative Verse of Charles Wesley* (London, 1962); see also J. Ernest Rattenbury, *The Eucharistic Hymns of John and Charles Wesley* (London, 1948).

[116] Of these, three from Paulus Gerhardt, two each from Gerhard Tersteegen and John Scheffler, and one each from Ernst Lange, Joachim Lange, J. A. Rothe, J. H. Schein, and J. J. Winckler still survive in *The Methodist Hymn Book* (1933). For the *Collection* see *Works*, vol. 7.

[117] E.g., 'IV. Sing *lustily* and with good courage. . . . Be no more afraid of your voice now, nor more ashamed of its being heard, than when you sung the songs of Satan. . . . VI. Sing *in time*. Whatever time is sung, be sure to keep with it. Do not run before, nor stay

preaching, so also he denounced repetitiveness in hymns, anthems, and oratorios.[118] In the *Minutes* for 1768 (Q. 23) he deplores 'the repeating the same word so often (but especially while another repeats different words, the horrid abuse which runs through the modern church music); as it shocks all common sense, so it necessarily brings in dead formality, and has no more of religion in it than a Lancashire hornpipe'.[119] The relevance of all this for our purposes is that when Wesley sprinkled his sermons with hymn stanzas or couplets, as he did generously, he could count on hearers and readers who could respond to them from their own experiences.

---

behind it, but attend close to the leading voices, and move therewith as exactly as you can. And take care you sing not *too slow*. This drawling way naturally steals on all who are lazy, and it is high time to drive it out from among us, and sing all our tunes just as quick as we did at first.'

See also, *Minutes*, 1765: 'Q. [28]: What can be done to make the people sing better? A. (1) Teach them to sing by note, and to sing our tunes first. (2) Take care they do not sing too slow. (3) Exhort all that can, in every congregation, to sing. (4) Set them right that sing wrong. Be patient therein.'

[118] See JWJ, Aug. 9, 1768: 'I . . . was greatly disgusted at the manner of singing [at Neath, where the choir] repeated the same words, contrary to all sense and reason, six or eight or ten times over . . . '; see also Mar. 19, 1778: 'In the evening, I preached at Pebworth church; but I seemed out of my element. A long anthem was sung; but I suppose none beside the singers could understand one word of it. Is not that "praying in an unknown tongue"? I could no more bear it in any church of mine than Latin prayers.' See also Apr. 8, 1781: 'The service was at the usual hours. I came just in time to put a stop to a bad custom, which was creeping in here; a few men, who had fine voices, sang a psalm which no one knew, in a tune fit for an opera, wherein three, four, or five persons sang different words at the same time! What an insult upon common sense! What a burlesque upon public worship! No custom can excuse such a mixture of profaneness and absurdity.'

[119] See the full answer to Q. 39 ('How shall we guard against formality in public worship? Particularly in singing?') in the Large *Minutes*, 1780.

6. ON READING WESLEY'S SERMONS

Wesley was not born a great preacher, nor did he come by his fame as a preacher by diligence alone. It was, in effect, thrust upon him by an unfolding succession of events in which he was always more reactor than actor. What is crucial, from the very beginning of the Revival, was that it was Wesley's message that counted for more than his manner, and this suggests a basic reference point in reading him. John Donne's sermons are aural feasts that delight the ear, stir the imagination, and move the heart; but they are most fully savoured when read aloud with a practiced actor's eye for word-play and nuance. Wesley's rhetoric is markedly different. There are only occasional flights of eloquence in them—all short. Wesley's message is Wesley's medium—it is a transaction with a reader responding to insights springing from shared traditions and a shared source in Holy Writ. The typical Wesley sermon begins with a brief proemium promptly followed by an expository 'contract' between the preacher and the reader ('I am to show . . .', etc.). The reader is thus entitled to judge between the preacher's intention and his performance.[1] And always, it is the 'application' on which the whole effort is focused; this makes most of the sermons intensely personal and practical.[2] Wesley was content that others might be more exciting if he could be more nourishing.

None of his sermons stands alone; none is norm for all the others. Wesley can quite readily be quoted against himself when this passage or that is taken out of context. His sermons are bound to be misread unless they are understood as experimental statements and restatements of his vision of the Christian life. On first scanning they may seem repetitious:

---

[1] That Wesley honoured this compact in the breach as well as in the observance may be seen, e.g., in Sermon 39, 'Catholic Spirit' (where the text is merely a pretext) or in the following folkloric anecdote from Scotland (where the standards of 'sermon-tasting' were higher than in England): 'In one of Wesley's visits to Dunbar, when preaching in the open air [and rambling], a young man in the crowd cried, "Stick to your text.". . . Wesley was so much confounded as if a thunderbolt had fallen at his feet, . . . struck dumb with astonishment, and had not a word to say. After a little, he went on with his discourse in a much less confident tone than formerly;' quoted from the *Berwickshire News*, Oct. 26, 1883, in *WHS* 17 (1930):146–47.

[2] See Wesley's letter to Joseph Taylor, Feb. 14, 1787: 'A sermon should be all application.' See also Sermons 20, *The Lord Our Righteousness*, §II.20; and 5, 'Justification by Faith', §IV.9 and n.

one quickly comes to recognize favourite phrases, quotations—some of his illustrations are pressed into double duty. And yet, even such repetitions have their purpose: they represent Wesley's way of trying to expose old truths in new lights.

Wesley's sermons may be read in gulps, without the distraction of notes. Or, they may be savoured and probed, and this is more fruitful as one becomes more deeply immersed in their backgrounds. They can be read in different sequences or in topical clusters (as, e.g., the pivotal series on Law and Gospel in the thirteen sermons 'Upon Our Lord's Sermon on the Mount', Sermons 31–33, together with the three following, Sermons 34–36). There is no doubt that the sermons in *Sermons 1–4* stand as a bloc and that, together, they do define the evangelical substance of Wesley's message. But they do not display its entire breadth and range, and it is unfortunate that conventional preoccupations with them have encouraged a corresponding neglect of the corpus *as a whole*. Thus Wesley's stature as a theologian has been casually underestimated, by Methodists and non-Methodists alike; his oversimplifications have been taken too easily at face value, and not recognized as hints of a more resourceful mind than meets the eye. Reverence for him as cult-hero and patriarch in Methodism has not preserved Methodist theology from serious distortions in the course of its post-Wesleyan developments.[3] Methodists, therefore, have almost as much to gain from genuinely critical studies of Wesley (from his own sources and as a whole) as do his fellow Anglicans and other Christians of every persuasion. It is, however, equally misleading to handle Wesley's sermons chiefly as historical curios. He was no antiquarian himself, and he would scorn any proposal that his sermons should ever be turned into puzzlers for pedants. Their real test is in their continuing power of witness—the possibility that their essential message may be updated and reformulated, again and again, while generations succeed each other.

The heart of Wesley's gospel was always its lively sense of God's grace at work at every level of creation and history in persons and communities. He took the 'Protestant principle' for granted: that God alone is God, with no rivals in creation save those idols that make human pride the primal font of sin and self-delusion. But he also cherished the Greek Christian heritage as a needful balance and, most especially, in its understanding of the Holy

---

[3] Robert E. Chiles, *Theological Transition in American Methodism* (Nashville, 1965), provides a survey of the shallow roots of American Methodism in Wesleyan theology. See also Franz Hildebrandt, *From Luther to Wesley* (London, 1951), for an example of how Wesley may be 'Lutheranized'. But see Garth Lean, *John Wesley, Anglican* (London, 1964), for a fresh perspective.

Spirit as the mediator of all graces—sufficient grace in all, irresistible grace in none. His ecclesiology turned on the conviction that all the means of grace are the Spirit's gifts to the priesthood of all believers and, under the Spirit's guidance, to a representative priesthood.[4] The 'catholic substance' of Wesley's theology is the theme of *participation*—the idea that all life is of grace and all grace is the mediation of Christ by the Holy Spirit. Wesley did not, of course, invent any of these ideas, but neither did he find them already compounded in the special syndrome that he struggled for and largely achieved.[5]

Moreover, if his theology was unsystematic by design, this was not because of his disdain for coherence. After all, he was a trained logician and much more of a rationalist than the pietists among his followers have ever recognized. And yet, from his knowledge of the history of Christian doctrine he was aware of the fate of theological systems; besides, he himself had been bred up in a tradition with fewer experiments in 'systematic theology', as such, than any other. He had, therefore, come to take it for granted that the ways to Christian wisdom cannot be mapped as neatly as one might wish. The Christian pilgrim's progress is more securely guided by controlling insights (themselves works of the Spirit) than by manuals or treatises or *summae*.

By the same token, if Wesley's theology is ecumenical in scope and spirit, this was not the product of a pliant disposition. He was a very strong-minded man, scarcely fazed by criticism. He rarely changed his mind under anything short of circumstances that he could recognize as providential. He could, and often did, provoke controversy; he never backed away from a debate; his store of oil for troubled waters was meagre. It is all the more remarkable, therefore, that such a man could see so clearly the positive values of valid pluralism in an age when dogmatism and indifferentism were posed as the only two live options. Actually, Wesley's ecumenical vision was less relevant in his own age than it may have since become. He was only dimly aware, even as his movement grew, that the *fides historica* had already begun to lose its grip upon the European mind.[6]

---

[4] See 'Disciplinary' *Minutes*, Aug. 3, 1745 (*Qs.* 1-9), and the 'points of discipline', discussed in mid-morning of June 15, 1747 (*Qs.* 1-14).

[5] See George, *London Life*, p. 269, for a comment on how relevant Wesley's peculiar doctrine of assurance would have been in its own special time.

[6] See Peter Gay, *The Enlightenment* (p. 35, n. 55 above). See also Carl L. Becker, *The Heavenly City of the Eighteenth Century Philosophers* (New Haven, 1959). For a Christian historian's celebration of the end of the history of dogma, see Adolf von Harnack, *Grundriss der Dogmengeschichte*, 2 vols. (Freiburg, 1889-1901), and *Das Wesen Des Christentums* (Leipzig, 1900).

He would have been uneasy with the salvaging efforts of Schleiermacher and Ritschl; he would have been horrified by the disintegrations of Strauss and Feuerbach. By the same token, though, he would have deplored all fundamentalist oppositions between the Christian tradition and 'contemporary culture'. One may honestly suppose, however, that he would have rejoiced at the surprises of the Spirit in the modern ecumenical movement, and in the new flood of Christian charity let loose in the world by Pope John XXIII and the Second Vatican Council.

The Christian tradition remains in every age to be rediscovered and transvaluated—an inexhaustible resource for new horizons of inquiry and venture.[7] Wesley's sermons deserve a place in that tradition and deserve more careful appraisal by historians and theologians than they have had. By the same token, though, John Wesley merits a closer look by those 'plain people' he loved so dearly and who, as he was so well aware, 'are competent judges of those truths which are necessary to their present and future happiness'.[8]

---

[7] See Albert C. Outler, *The Christian Tradition and the Unity We Seek* (New York, 1957).

[8] *Sermons*, Preface, §2, in *Works*, 1:104.

Printed in the United States
42852LVS00004B/334